An Author's Guide to Writing a Book

Writing Blueprint

Writing Blueprint

Chosen Destiny Books

Copyright 2018

Donna Christopher

All rights reserved. No part of this book may be used or reproduced by any means, graphic, electronic or mechanical, including photocopying, recording, taping or by any informational storage retrieval system without the written permission of the publisher except in the case of brief quotations embodied in critical articles and reviews.

For information please contact the author at DonnaChristopherAuthor@gmail.com
Social media @donnachristopherauthor

Write your book in 27 days with outlining and consistent writing!

A Note From The Author

So, you want to write a book? Well, welcome to the Writers Blueprint, a guide for writers to learn how to write a book efficiently and effectively by outlining and using your outline as your guide to write your book from idea to completion. As a writer myself, a published author with twenty plus years' experience, I found outlining to be the best method for me to write and complete a book again and again while perfecting my gift of writing. This is also the method I use when I work with clients teaching them how to write and complete their book. When I mentor aspiring authors, I also guide them to write their book using the outlining method. I am so excited to be sharing my knowledge and experience with you, to help you complete your book by using the outlining method. I encourage you to read each section before completing each exercise in the process. You will learn the importance of each section and how it can help when writing your book.

Have you ever said to yourself "I have writers block," and felt like you were stuck? Was your book left unfinished, maybe even untouched for days, weeks, months, or years even? Do you know you want to write a book, but just don't know where to start? Do you have a great idea for a book, but just don't know how to develop your idea? Well, learning to write by using an outlining method will help you fight the mindset that makes you feel like you have "writers block" or want to walk away feeling defeated before you even start the process. Outlining will help you overcome the feeling of not knowing what to write or where to start. Using the methods in this book will help you write consistently and efficiently without wondering what to write next, where your story is going, and how it will start and end. Your idea will be clear when you use your outline as your blueprint.

Outlining will also allow you to write your book easier with a more organized plan, and more efficiently than doing so without outlining. Some experts may be able to write a book without outlining one piece of their book, and maybe even write their book in no time at all, then send it straight to their editors. But most writers are not that good, even if they were just that good, why not use a blueprint designed to help aspiring and existing authors to become the best writer they can be. Outlining is the planning you do before you take the writing journey.

Not only is outlining designed to help write the book inside of you waiting to burst out on paper, but it serves as a good reference when writing sequels, when you need to refresh your mind on key details about your story or characters without having to scroll back through all the written pages in your book to find what you are looking for. Taking it a step further, if you decide to turn your book into a script for a movie, you will have all the key details available in your outline to get you started.

There are so many benefits to outlining your book before you write your book. That is why I wanted to write a book for Authors, aspiring and existing, to guide them through the outlining process, but to also give instructions as to why, how, and what about each part of the writing process. Why not create a blueprint for your book to help you write your book? Why not create a blueprint just in case you need to go back and reference what you wrote about without reading the book all over again? Why not create a blueprint for your book to help you write more efficiently? Why not create and use a blueprint to help you when writing a sequel, or a script if and when you decide to turn your book into a sequel or your script into a movie?

My first book I ever wrote started with pen and paper, writing down all my thoughts and ideas. My ideas were all over the place. I started creating categories for my characters jotting down notes everywhere to describe who they were and why they were important for my story. I created categories for chapter titles that I now call my chapter table of contents, for plots and twist, key points and even summaries of characters, chapters and my entire story. Before I knew it, I was outlining and didn't even realize it. Once I did realize, I started to organize each component until I had a process that I could use and still use today.

Every time I was asked, "how do you start writing a book," I started rambling off every detail how I start writing my books. Although some got it, some didn't get it until I took them step by step how to do it. I got it of course as I created my method, but every time I helped someone else, it showed me where others struggled and what areas they needed more help with when they didn't know how to start the writing process at all.

Step by step is where I take you, the writer, on the writing journey from one author to another, using an outlining method that has worked for me and countless others that I have coached on their writing journey. I am so glad you are here! So glad you are taking this journey, becoming a step closer to making your dreams of completing your book, becoming an author or repeat author, a reality!

Outlining is everything to me, and with every book I write, I go through the same process. I practice what I preach with every book.

Outlining is great for all types of writers and becomes an amazing tool for authors. It becomes your blueprint for future writing, like spark notes for a book you don't have time to read before starting a new project. I hope you enjoy this process just as much as I do using this method every time I outline book after book and just as much as I do teaching this process and watching as my clients successfully write their books. Don't forget to pay it forward and tell someone else about this book if it indeed has helped you like I know it will. This book explains the writing process and gives you pages to start outlining your book. For future projects you can purchase "Writing Blueprint - The Outlining Journal" that consist of blank pages for you to outline like the pro you will become. Happy learning, happy outlining! Now go slay those writing goals!

Follow me for more information, writing tips, and email me your thoughts and comments.

@donnachristopherauthor on IG & Facebook
Twitter: @donnachristophr
Periscope: Donna Christopher
E-mail: donnachristopherauthor@gmail.com
Website: donnachristopherauthor.com

How to Use This Book

If you are anything like me you have already flipped through the pages and now anxious, excited, and ready to start your writing journey. That is exactly how you should feel as an aspiring author and also as an existing author. With every book the writing journey brings an amazing feeling mixed with all types of emotions and feelings going on inside your mind and body. But starting a new writing journey brings the same feeling with every book, even if it is your first or your twentieth book written, the feeling of excitement mixed with anxiety is there.

When I was just a little girl I had a fascination with paper, pens and the creativity of telling a great story. My imagination was crazy amazing and everyone and everything inspired me to write poetry, short stories, stuff that didn't or wouldn't make sense to anyone else but me. It was my escape, my enjoyment and what I later in life found out was my passion and my purpose.

With over 20 years of writing experience, and over 15 years of professionally writing, my expertise in what it takes to write a well-written book has become a valuable tool for me and others that cross my path acquiring my services. I decided that although what I know now comes natural to me, there are so many other aspiring authors and existing authors who can benefit from the knowledge between these pages. Years ago, when I wrote my first book, I had nothing to help me become a great writer. What I have learned and shared here in these pages would have been "a writers" dream for me when I wrote my first book, like winning the writing lottery. My goal is for you to be able to relate as a writer or aspiring writer, and use the content given here to write your very own master plan to use when writing your very own book.

Using the knowledge given here will increase your planning and organization and help you pull out the details needed to write your book from start to finish, from an outline to a completed manuscript. I compiled everything I have learned about outlining, that has worked for me over and over in hopes to help as many aspiring authors birth their books, making their dream of becoming a published author a reality and to help as many existing authors write their book easier, more efficiently and effectively so they too can continue to birth great books and write amazing stories.

Feel free to share your progress and success with me by emailing me at donnachristopherauthor@gmail.com and don't forget to follow me on Instagram @donnachristopherauthor and twitter @donnachristophr I would love to hear from you!

So, are you ready to partake in the writing journey?

Great, now let's get started!

Let's discuss how to use this book. First thing first, believe that you can, and you will write this book. There is not a doubt in my mind that if you want to write a book, YOU CAN! First thing we will cover is how to get your mindset right, to believe and know that writing your book is something that is possible if you follow the steps in this process. Start thinking about your "why," why do you want to write a book and what will be the purpose of your book.

This book will help you think about your "Idea" and develop your idea further to help you write great content. So, don't fear if you don't know where to start, we will be discussing different ways to help you develop your idea(s). You have more to your idea than you know, you just need to think through the pieces of your idea and write down as much as you can so that you can see the bigger picture and pull your ideas out and together.

Brainstorming, research, commitment and planning, are all very important in the process and we will discuss and plan to do each of these components. Get your mind set right now on how committed you want to be in order to get your book written and completed. You can do this!

We will also discuss the outlining process and why each component in the process is so important. Outlining can be a simple process or a complex process depending on what methods work best for you. I will be discussing everything that I know about the entire process and after you go through the entire process, you can then decide what method works best for you or create a middle method that you can use in your writing process that works better for you. My hope is that you will go through the entire process before you decide. Don't worry, there are extra blank pages in the back of the book for you to use in addition to what we will be using to learn the process. After you complete the process, you can decide what part of the process to continue using and what you don't think you need to keep using if that is the case. Each component in the process plays an important part for your story development. Some people may only desire to create a simple outline, while others, like myself, love the more detailed process that completely develops your story so all you have to do is write the book from your outline and fill in the missing details. Some of the topics we will be learning about in the outlining process are:

Summarizing
Key points
Character Development

Time Capsule
Chapter Development
Plot Development
Scene/Setting Development
Sequel Setup
Writing your first chapter
27 Day writing challenge specifically for you
Frequently Asked Questions Answered
Overcoming Writer's Block
and so much more...

I am so excited that you are dedicating your time to learn more about how to write a book using an outlining method to help you write an amazing book of your own that you can be proud of. If you follow the steps here you will find that getting your book done will be an accomplishment, a slayed goal, a dream coming true that is closer than you may have imagined. So, keep reading, and keep learning about the process. I hope you enjoy this book as much as I enjoyed writing, teaching the process, and educating you along the way. Read each section and then try to complete the worksheets that follow each section. The written assignments will all become a part of your outline.

The first step is for you to write who this book belongs to and if you don't already know, start brainstorming on a title for your book and a subtitle if you decide you want to use one. It's not etched in stone anywhere that you must have a sub title, some people choose to have one to enhance their book title. It's your choice. But create a working title for now that stands out and fits your book. Make it interesting, eye catching and ear catching, one that will make people think about and want to purchase your book. You will use your title often as you write your book. We will discuss more about this later but giving your project a name makes it feel real. The title can be your permanent book title or a temporary filler. Stat thinking about what to call your book now.

Start brainstorming on an Author name you want to use for your book. You can use your real name or choose to use a pen name - a name that you make up, that you want your fans to call you, that you want people to reference you by. This is a chance to create that superstar name you always wanted. Depending on what you are writing about, this may play a role in what name you decide to use. Some use their first and middle name. Some may use one name only. Others use first initials and then a last name. Do you want people to know you are a female or a male? Others may use a name that is totally made up. This name, your name, will stick with you so start brainstorming and choose wisely. Your fans will call you this name when they meet you. Your friends and family will start to call you this name. Make sure it is a name that you can tolerate being called.

Your name nor your title will be concrete until you actually publish. So brainstorm, be creative, and know that at any time before you publish you can make changes. On the next page, give yourself a working project title. This can be the title of your book or a name that sums up what you are writing until you come up with a title. You choose what to name your project. Write in the start date, the day your project begins will be the day you start to write your book when your outline has been completed. Also, give yourself a completion date. This is the day you desire or plan to be completed with your project. Be realistic with yourself. If you know you will make time to write consistently then plan your 27-day writing journey. If you know you will not have much time during a week, then plan accordingly. If you make writing a priority, you can write your book in 27-days or less. Next, complete the title page and write in your potential author name or pen name. You can add this information at any time while completing your outline. Remember, you can change your title or name at any point until you are ready to publish.

Each section will explain what needs to be done and why that section is important. This process is designed to help you think about what you are writing so that you can write your book like you imagined. This book is also designed to help you pull out all your great ideas. This process will show you how to develop each component of your story so that you will have your very own blueprint before you start to actually write your masterpiece, your story, your book! Follow the directions in each section and you will be on your way to outlining like a boss.

This is the beginning of your book being completed. I am so excited to be a part of your writing journey, and I am so excited that you took this step to learn more and do more to make your writing journey fun, amazing, and easier.

Now let's go!

Project Title

_____

_____

_____

_____

_____

_____

Start Date_____

Completion Date_____

7 Phases Before Writing

Mindset
1. Get Your mind right! Know WHY you are writing your book and know that if you desire to write a book and you believe that you can, then you can! YES, YOU CAN write an amazing story that you too can be proud of. Get your mind focused on writing an amazing book!

Idea
2. Your idea is great, start developing and expanding on that idea so that you can create interesting content to write about that will attract and keep the attention of your readers! There is no wrong idea, every idea you have can serve a purpose for that amazing story you will write! Every great book starts with an idea!

Brainstorm
3. Great ideas, great story plots, and great content comes from brainstorming. Brainstorm on everything about your story and use this process to help you come up with even more great ideas that will make your story better. Brainstorm before and during the writing process.

Research
4. Researching key items in your story helps when it comes to you sounding knowledgeable about the topics you are discussing. Research is a key component to making sure your story flow and making sure your readers can relate. You always want to make sure you sound qualified to talk about whatever it is you write about.

Commitment Plan
5. Being consistent and committed to your writing is very important to getting your book done. A commitment plan that you can execute is essential to writing and completing your book. Commit to plan and plan to commit. Stay committed and your book will be complete in no time at all.

Summarize
6. Summarize your story and your ideas. Write everything down that you want to include in your book. You never want to forget what you wanted to say. Summarizing your story is a great reference for you to write your book without missing important information. Your summary becomes a part of your outline.

Outlining
7. Outlining is a very important key component to writing a book efficiently. This phase of writing will be your blueprint once you start to write your book. Look at it as your road map to writing. Even if you take a detour or make a few stops, your outline, also known as your blueprint, will be your guide to help you stay on track, and have fun on your writing journey to finishing your book. During this phase it will include your summary and you will develop your characters, your story plots and so much more. This will make writing your book from your outline worth every moment of planning. Outline like a boss so you can write like a boss, flawlessly!

This Book Belongs to

_____

Author Name (Pen Name)
Potential

_____
_____
_____
_____
_____

Book Title & Sub Title
Potential

_____
_____
_____
_____
_____

Mindset - Knowing your WHY

How is your mindset when it comes to you thinking about making your dreams become a reality? Do you believe that your dreams will come true? Do you believe that you can actually do what needs to be done to make your dreams your reality? Believing and knowing that whatever you can imagine to be, CAN BE is half the journey of making your dreams a realty. So, do you believe in yourself? Think about it for a moment. Your dreams are yours. Your dreams are meant to come true!

When you think about writing a book, can you see the finished book in your hands with your name across the front;

Written by _____ (you)?

Take a moment and visualize that very situation. Believe that one day soon, with the help of this book to properly plan your writing journey, your book will be completed, published, and in your hands!

Dream an amazing dream that belongs to you and know that whatever you dream, whatever you desire to be in life, YES it can be! Change your mindset to a "yes I can, I do believe, I know it can happen for me" and watch how much more successful you will become at making your dreams become reality! Change your mindset, change your life! Believe that you can and just do what needs to be done to start your journey making dreams come true. Start here with this book and believing in yourself enough to know that your book will be written by you, and one day, sooner than later, your finished book will be published for the world to read and you will be holding a copy in your hands!

The next thing I want you to think about is your why. Why do you want to write this book? Think about your reason for wanting to write a book. Do you want to help people? Motivate them through your words, your story? Do you intend to teach someone, or simply entertain? Do you just want to become an author and maybe make a lot of money from writing? Whatever your why is, think about it and write your why statement on the next page. Know your why and let that be a guiding factor as to why you complete your book.

I started my writing career wanting to write a book so that I can see my story in print, something that I created, wrote, and published inside a book. I loved writing as far back as I can remember, and I still love to write now. I soon came to realize that I actually had a gift of story-telling and a gift to write. People around me purchased and read my book and started to praise me for a job well done. I loved the feeling that I received knowing that people were motivated, inspired, touched with love, laughter or simply given hope by something I wrote. It felt good. No, it felt great!

So, why do I want to write a book? My answer today would be different than what my answer would have been back in 2005 when I wrote my first book. But today I would say, to entertain and inspire people through the different messages I incorporate into my stories without taking away from the story itself, to teach others what I would have wanted to know, knowing what I know now, and to share knowledge with people who could benefit from what I have learned, knowledge that would otherwise be hidden in my mind. I still aspire to write amazing stories and entertain my readers, but if I could help someone to have a better life, to give them hope, to motivate them to want more, be better, or change their life for the better, that is a major part of my why.

Writing this book is a part of my why, to help aspiring and existing writers wanting to write and publish their book without saying they have "writers block," or shelving their project because they don't know what to write next. So entertaining and helping people through my words is my why!

Think about your why, write down your why, believe in your why. Know that if it matters to you, it will matter to someone else who is waiting on you to write and publish your book. Don't wait. Start your writing journey now. Write your "Why Statement "and make sure that your mindset is set on believing that you can. I believe that you can. I know that you can. So, plan your writing here in these pages and write an amazing story that aligns with your why!

Why Statement

Why Statement

Idea

What is your idea for this amazing book you want to write? How do you expand on these ideas to know and understand what you will write about? The idea phase hinders a lot of people from writing their book because they don't understand how to pull their ideas together to make sense enough to write a story worthy enough to read. If any part of the above statement is you, it's ok, you are on the right path using this book to learn how to outline. Your idea can be developed if you just start writing down all the pieces of the writing puzzle.

On the next two pages I want you to start writing down your ideas, even if they don't make sense to anyone else but you. This book is for you and no one else needs to see what you write unless YOU give them permission to do so. Start writing the first ides that come to your mind and keep writing every idea, every spoken word you want your characters to speak, any scene that you need to paint. Your ideas all play a part in your story and you know what you want it to be about and what you want it to say. You just need to pull those great ideas from your mind to paper.

The purpose of you writing down your ideas is to help you build your story, but also to help you remember that great idea that you could otherwise forget if you do not write it down. Start writing your ideas down on paper as they come to you no matter where you are. Use the note section in your phone if you don't have access to pen and paper or a computer. If you were to be interviewed by someone regarding your idea for your book, where would you start? What would be the first thing you tell them your book will be about? Do you know what you want to happen first? What kind of twist will happen? What about characters, do you know you want a "boy meets girl" situation? Or maybe you want a murder to take place? What about your main characters, what do you plan for their purpose in the story to be? Do you know how you want it to end? These are similar questions you should be asking yourself to help pull out all the great ideas you have inside your mind. Explore every angel to enhance your story, making sure you write the best book you can imagine.

Think about all the interesting events you want to take place in your story and write every idea you have down on paper. You can later start pulling your ideas together to create and write your masterpiece of a story, one idea at a time! Let's go through a few scenario's regarding Idea's that need to be explored a bit more to pull out your great ideas.

In my book "Love Never Fails," I knew I needed my main male character to portray his life as a homeless man, even though he was a millionaire. I needed him to find his true love while on his journey portraying to being homeless. But in order for me to write this story and make it believable and amazing I needed a concept as to why he was portraying himself as a homeless man in the first place. This is where I had to use my creative imagination and create a storyline that led up to this happening. So, what did I do?

I gave him a fiancée who he thought would be his wife, but he also had a doubting feeling about her truly loving him for him, and not for all the money and material things he had. So, I setup a scenario where he would find out about her cheating on him. This led to heart break and a mind shift that led to him portray his life living as a homeless man. His purpose was to see how people would treat him not knowing who he was or what he had. I knew how he would get there and I now had a new plot to help the story flow. Now I needed some filler ideas for my story.

I needed to figure out how the pieces would come together. What role will the ex-fiancée play in keeping this relationship from going forward. Would she fight to get her man back? Would she try to eliminate future competition? What other characters would I need to create to intertwine with my main characters and help the story to be perfect? What would their story be? These are all questions I would ask myself and more to create my story, my characters, their purpose, the plots, twist, to help me think of any key points, scenes that need to happen, words that need to be said and so on.

So, as you are writing your Idea Statement, write down everything you can think about that would make sense in your story. Characters needed, scenes that need to happen to make your story come together and any important facts you can come up with that need to be included. Your ideas only need to make sense to you. So, let's get started writing down all of YOUR ideas that will lead to your amazing story written in your book! Remember the only idea that is not good is that which is forgotten because it was never written.

Idea Statement

Idea Statement

Brainstorm

Now it is time to brainstorm on your ideas. This section is where you need to write down any one-off words, statements, scenes, plot ideas, things that you are not sure if it would make sense, different endings, different setups, etc. Brainstorm on your ideas and think about different scenarios to your story. If you added a certain character would it change the outcome and make your story better? How can you setup the suspense to keep your readers wondering what happens next, keep them wanting more of the story?

What about inspirational messages in your story? What do you want your readers to take away from your story? Where will you incorporate this lesson and how will you set the message up to flow without making it seem like you are preaching a sermon, unless that's what you intend to do. Brainstorm different opportunities to deliver what you want to say. Someone experienced a heart break and a friend telling them how trifling that type of woman is. Or a mother comforting her son or daughter giving them a scripture from the bible and comforting words. What about a drug addict, prostitute, abusive person, or the one being abused, finding help through a therapist, preacher, or someone who was in their shoes, maybe you can deliver a message through them.

Does someone die? What will be the key details to how they died and who will be involved? Does it make sense? Does it need to be a mystery? Brainstorm on different ways to let your readers know this person is about to die, may die, could die. Do your readers need to have an "OH NO" feeling when leading up to the killing? Should your readers if they are a bit sensitive feel the urge to cry? Or is someone sick and dying? Does the family know? Who will be affected the most? Will this be a sad moment for many? Will someone be happy about this death? What type of weapon or disease will cause the death. Think about what will make your story better with each plot, and character, and start to build each scene.

Brainstorm on whatever it is you think needs more developing in your story. This keeps you thinking about the development of your story before you start to build your characters and your chapters that lead to you writing your amazing story! Let's get to brainstorming!

Brainstorm

Brainstorm

Research

As you are expanding your ideas and brainstorming how to make your story better, write down any piece of your story that you may need to research. Is it a medication you need to know details about that someone is taking? What about a drug that someone is addicted to that makes them act a certain way, overdose on, make them horny. Maybe someone is shot and in a coma. Where would they have to get shot to cause a coma? Would they have to lose a lot of blood or what? Research any details in your story that you need to be sure is accurate to make that part believable when you are writing about it.

Will there be therapist sessions? What kinds of questions do they ask? What about a doctor diagnosing someone with cancer or some other disease, what will they say in the doctor's office when they reveal the bad news, how will they say it? What symptoms will they have?

Research names of wine, liquor or something particular that you mention in the story. How many drinks to make someone pass out, get alcohol poisoning and so on. No matter what it is you are writing about unless it is intended to be a mystery or "unreal," you want to make sure you are sounding like you have knowledge about that subject.

As you complete different sections of this book, think about what you need to research, write down one word or a phrase of words and come back to this section when you are ready to sit down and do your research. Then write down your findings to refer back to when needed as you are writing the book. The internet is your friend, so use it to help you make your story better. Become an expert on what you are writing about or at least research enough to know what you are talking about and make everyone else reading believe that you are an expert.

This shouldn't take up too much of your time but will become a huge benefit for you when writing your book and add to the amazing story you are about to write!

Research

Research

Summarize

When you start to summarize your story, start by writing down all of your thoughts, from beginning to end how you envision your story will flow. Try to go in order of how you think your story will be written and summarize the events that will take place, including the plots that you already know will happen. Even if you don't have all of the details, write your summary to give enough information so that anyone reading your summary will know what your story is about.

You will develop your story at different stages of the process, but for this phase of your outline, you need to summarize your thoughts regarding what your story will be about. When I wrote Love Never Fails, I knew I wanted to start with a brief story about my main character Brielle reflecting on a piece of her past when she was abused by her ex-boyfriend who was also her children's father. I wanted my readers to know personal details about her journey of love, and how even though she kept her guard up and wasn't looking for love, she never closed her heart to the true love that God had for her. I wrote the details about this chapter to help me know about the reflection, how she was dreaming and woke up terrified needing to pray her fear away. This was also another entrance into her life, her past, who she was, what she had been through.

If I needed to add a key detail about her or another character that was affected by something in chapter one, I would add a simple note like, ex-boyfriend will escape from jail and try to come back to be with Brielle. You can write as much as you need in your summary to help you reference what your initial thoughts are and any details you want to be sure to include in your story. When I write my summaries, they are anywhere from 2 pages to 10 pages of details about what I plan to write.

This information may change as you start to write your outline and your story. The main goal here is to write down your initial thoughts about your story. A starting place to get you thinking of what you are going to write about, and in what chapter order. This will give you an idea how you can start developing your story chapter by chapter to make it flow and to make it amazing!

Story Summary

Story Summary

Story Summary

Story Summary

Story Summary

Commitment & Planning

Are you ready to commit yourself and your time to writing your book? The key to writing is commitment and consistency. You have to find time each day, or several days in your week, to dedicate yourself to writing your book. Yes, this includes time out of your busy day to write but it also includes a writing space. You must find a space where you can write where no one can bother you or at least minimize the distractions.

I have children and a husband who seem to always need momma/wifey. They know how important they are to me, but they also know how important it is for me to be able to write with minimum disturbance. Sometimes it is harder for me to concentrate in the afternoons when they are out of school, off work, when they are full of energy, hungry, and missed me while they were away. So, I know at that time of day would not be ideal for me to write without disturbance. You must find the best time for you. Discuss your plans for writing your book with your family, tell them what you are trying to accomplish and what you need from them to be able to make your dreams become a reality! You may be surprised just how supportive they will be.

When I sat down and wrote out everything that I do or could possibly do in a day/week, then added up the time it took, I was able to realistically see how much time I actually had to write each day/week. Next is a worksheet I used for myself to help me get to the number of hours I had available each week. So, add up your time, think about everything you do being realistic with yourself. If you watch television, add that in. Gossip on the phone, add that in. Hang out with your friends every Friday night, add that in. This is your book so be real with yourself. Now if it is something you don't want anyone to know that just may happen to pick up your book and read it, use code words or simply say me time, extra, or something unique that you want to use.

If you find that you don't have any time to write, this is when you would look at your schedule and see what could be taken out of your schedule. You must make sacrifices like not watching TV, taking a break from going out, so that you can make time to write and make your dreams come true. After you know how much time you have, then you can start to plan your week of writing!

Commitment & Planning

Build Your Time Schedule

_____ Hours of sleep every night – Approximate average

_____ Hours of School/Work prep –morning/night, yourself and your children

_____ Hours of television – Weekly shows, other people watching TV that you get caught up in, Movies & etc.

_____ Hours of Relax "Me" time – Baths, naps, chill, phone, social media (non-working time), etc.

_____ Hours of Football/Basketball Time or other sports - kids practice to and from time, Game Day, watching sports, NBA/NFL on or going to games.

_____ Hours of 9-5 job or whatever your full time or part time job hours are. Include travel time there and back.

_____ Hours of spouse time. Don't include time already added for movies, chill time or any event that you two may be at together already listed above.

_____ Hours of kid time for whatever they need; help with homework, cook, etc. This is in addition to the time spent with them while doing other stuff such as school prep, football time, tv time, etc.

_____ Other time allotted for specifics in your life add here

_____

_____

_____

_____

_____

_____

_____

_____

_____

_____ Add the above numbers together to come up with your total. Add it below.

_____ This is your total Hours of Occupied time in a week. Above totals.

168 hours (7-day work week total hours) - (minus) Total Occupied Hours = _____ hours.

This is how many hours remaining in your week that you can dedicate to your writing and accomplishing your dreams of publishing a book. Think about the time you mentioned above that is dedicated to other items. Besides sleep, unless it's more than 8 hours a night, think of what you can exclude to give yourself more time to write.

When multi-tasking with the time above, you could find additional time to add to your week to make time to write consistently. Any idol time is additional time that can be used towards your dream. Down town at work, sitting, waiting at practice, etc. So now you have an idea of how much time you have available to commit to writing.

YOU HAVE APPROXIMATELY _____ HOURS A WEEK TO WRITE!

YOU HAVE APPROXIMATELY _____ HOURS A WEEK TO DEDICATE TO WRITING!

Commitment Pledge

I _____
am committing to write _____ hours a week and _____ days a week.

Anything above and beyond will be a bonus! I pledge to commit to my writing and commit to myself because I am worthy!

Signed_____

Outlining

**Simple Version
Versus
Complex Version**

Outlining is everything to me. It may seem overwhelming at first when you think about all the components that are included in outlining, but I assure you, the process is fun and very helpful in developing your story. Outlining can be complex or simple and depends on the individual and what their needs are for writing their book. Regardless of the need, some form of outlining is needed before the writing part starts. After going through this complete process, the individual writer will then be able to choose to do a simple or complex outlining process. I would advise going through the complete process before making your final decision for future writing projects.

Simple outlining can be as simple as writing down a summary of your book, deciding on what to include in your chapters by doing a chapter summary and building your characters, just to get your initial ideas down on paper. Some may only need the summary pages, character quick snapshot and the chapter summary pages. They may choose to develop their story as they write their book and just need to write down the very basic information to get them started. This may be a good strategy for some but may be confusing for others and lead to a book that is poorly written or under developed

If you don't completely develop your story and think about each component before writing, it could lead to you rewriting chapters, needing to add or change chapters and/or characters and this could be frustrating and cause one to put their book away to come back at a later date that may never come.

Outlining is very important in developing your story. After going through the complex process of outlining you should feel comfortable enough to write your book from beginning to end and not feel lost for words or have a need to say you have writers block. Writers block is simply poor planning and a complex outlining plan will surely have you writing your book effectively and efficiently.

Before you write one word of your story you want to make sure you know what you are writing about, who you are writing about, why you are writing about them, what will happen and how it will happen. You also need to know where the scenes will take place. How will your characters act? What will they look like? Think about your favorite movie for a moment. If you had to watch that same movie and everyone sounded alike, looked alike, dressed alike and all the scenes happened in the exact same place, would it still be your favorite movie? You enjoy that movie because of the story that was written, the plots that were developed, key points or moments in the movie that stood out to you, where the story took place and how the characters were developed.

Now you see how important it is to develop your story before you start to write your book so that your readers will fall in love with your book as if they were watching their favorite movie. You should always aim to write a story that you too would enjoy if you were reading it for the first time.

I spend so much time developing my story before I start to write. So many ideas come into my head about great stories, one after another, that i don't want to risk forgetting any details about. Even if I am in the middle of writing a book, I pause to outline for the new book or at least start the process by writing a summary of my ideas and any key points or characters that I already know I am including. You never want to forget that great idea by waiting, so keep a journal or invest in more writing journals like this one (Writing Blueprint – The Outlining

Journal book is also available with bank outlining pages for experienced writers). Either way write, write, write down all your great ideas and develop your story before writing.

Complex outlining includes;
Brainstorming your Idea, Summarizing, Key Points, Character Development, Time Capsule, Chapter Summary & Developing, Plot Development, Scene/Setting Development, Writing an amazing 1st Chapter, Sequel Setup, and a Writing Plan.

Of course, there will be other things you will need to do in the process to prepare yourself for your writing journey like getting your mindset fixed on writing and believing that you can write a book. Also, researching topics you are writing about and finding time and space to write consistently, committing your time each week.

I am so excited for you to write and complete your book and I am glad you decided to use this outlining process to write your very own book. Try to complete each step in this book and learn as much as you can about your story and your characters, and your book will write itself with the help of your fingers typing up your well-developed story from your outline. I hope you are having fun so far and will enjoy the rest of the outlining process!

Happy Outlining

Key Points

Key points are simply points that need to be made in your story, sayings that need to be said a certain way, scenes that need to happen a certain way, or whatever key detail you need to make sure you remember to write a certain way and/or include in your story.

Your key points can be a few words or a sentence or two to get you started. And for those that need more details, use your detailing sheets to expand on that point to make sure you remember every detail needed to get your point down on paper so that you won't forget any key details in your story.

This is a time for you to write down anything that may have been missed in the summary or idea stage but also a place that you can reference to refresh your mind about the key point you are trying to make in your story.

As you write down your key points this is also an additional developing stage, giving you more time to think about what will be included in your amazing story that you are closer to writing. You may come up with something more you would like to add to your story and that is perfectly ok. You want to develop as much of your story as you can before you start to write your book. This will keep you from starting and stopping and wishing you would have developed your story more before you started to actual write.

Write down your key points then develop any of those further on your key point details sheets. Think outside the box and keep on developing this amazing story you are closer to writing!

Key Point Snippets

➢ 1. _____
_____
_____
_____

➢ 2. _____
_____
_____
_____

➢ 3. _____
_____
_____
_____

➢ 4. _____
_____
_____
_____

➢ 5. _____
_____
_____
_____

➢ 6. _____
_____
_____
_____

➢ 7. _____
_____
_____
_____

➢ 8. _____
_____
_____
_____

➢ 9. _____
_____
_____
_____

Key Point Snippets

➢ 10. _____
_____
_____
_____

➢ 11. _____
_____
_____
_____

➢ 12. _____
_____
_____
_____

➢ 13. _____
_____
_____
_____

➢ 14. _____
_____
_____
_____

➢ 15. _____
_____
_____
_____

➢ 16. _____
_____
_____
_____

➢ 17. _____
_____
_____
_____

➢ 18. _____
_____
_____
_____

Key Point Snippets

➢ 19. _____
_____
_____
_____

➢ 20. _____
_____
_____
_____

➢ 21. _____
_____
_____
_____

➢ 22. _____
_____
_____
_____

➢ 23. _____
_____
_____
_____

➢ 24. _____
_____
_____
_____

➢ 25. _____
_____
_____
_____

➢ 26. _____
_____
_____
_____

➢ 27. _____
_____
_____
_____

Key Point Snippets

➢ 28. _____
_____
_____

➢ 29. _____
_____
_____

➢ 30. _____
_____
_____

➢ 31. _____
_____
_____

➢ 32. _____
_____
_____

➢ 33. _____
_____
_____

➢ 34. _____
_____
_____

➢ 35. _____
_____
_____

➢ 36. _____
_____
_____

Key Point Snippets

- 37. _____
  _____
  _____

- 38. _____
  _____
  _____

- 39. _____
  _____
  _____

- 40. _____
  _____
  _____

- 41. _____
  _____
  _____

- 42. _____
  _____
  _____

- 43. _____
  _____
  _____

- 44. _____
  _____
  _____

- 45. _____
  _____
  _____

Key Point Details

Key Point #

Key Point #

Key Point #

Key Point #

Key Point Details

Key Point #

Key Point #

Key Point #

Key Point #

Key Point Details

Key Point #

Key Point #

Key Point #

Key Point #

Key Point Details

Key Point #

Key Point #

Key Point #

Key Point #

Character Development

Character development is very important for your story to be a great success. Take your time and revisit your characters naming before you complete your final draft. Develop your characters well and make them all unique. Don't worry, changing their name all at once after the story has been written and before published will be easy to do if that is what you end up doing. You just want to be sure you are developing great characters with great names that align with your story! Google is your best friend to figuring out how to make any changes to your document.

Even though changing names is an easy task, this is a step that can be avoided if you take the time to develop your characters before writing your book. This step has several pieces to get to your final character table of contents that list all of your characters and their purpose in the same place.

1. Brainstorm character names and make them unique for you and your story. Pay attention to names sounding alike and starting with the same letter unless that is your intention. Think about nicknames, alter egos, last names if any of this applies. Be sure to think past the beginning of your story if the name has any significance to an important part of your story, or if you plan to write sequels. Naming your characters are very important when writing your story and/or stories.

2. Character Profile will be your character bible to reference for any details regarding your characters at any time during your writing. Developing your characters profile will help you get to know your characters well before you allow them to guide you in your writing journey. Develop every detail about your characters that you can think of and write down any key details that make your character relevant to your story. Your characters are the foundation of your story, so a well-developed character is your path for a well-developed story! For sub-characters that are not mentioned consistently throughout the book but are still important, use the quick snapshot character sheets.

3. Create a character table that reference each character with a brief description as to who they are in the story.

Example: Rhonda Smith - Main girl - a young naive runaway girl falls in love with a bad boy (Romeo Edmond's) he breaks her heart

Romeo Edmond's - Main guy - bad boy who doesn't fall in love, goes around hurting women until he hurts the one girl he realized he truly loves.

4. The character Relationship sheet is simply a way for you to look at all the character names together to see if you have too many confusing similarities or need to adjust your naming of characters. You don't want to have a family member name John and his brother name Johnathan, it's to similar and your readers could get confused while reading. Unless this is your intention to confuse your readers, otherwise having similar naming may be confusing and should be avoided.

Character development is critical to writing a great story. You don't want your characters sounding alike, looking alike, or acting alike. You want to develop unique characters that fit the role they were intended to be in your story.

So, take time to develop your characters thoroughly to the point that "your characters" will write the story for you. Allow your characters to create their identity in your head space so that when you are done creating them they will feel like a part of you because you know them that well. Then you can write your story as if you are writing the story of someone close to you that you really care about. We do care about our characters as writers and as readers. After all, they each are from your imagination so technically your characters are a part of you!

Develop great characters that will help you write a great story!

Character Name Brainstorm

| Last Names | Nick Names |

| Female Names | Male Names |

Character Profile

Name_____
Nick Name_____ Social Status _____
Age_____ Birthday_____
Height_____ Race _____ Sex_____
Weight_____ Religion_____

Body Type _____
_____
Body Assets (big butt, boobs,
muscular, basketball build, etc)_____
_____
_____
_____
Personality_____
_____
_____
Dress style _____
_____
Other _____
_____
_____

Lifestyle_____
Income class_____
House_____
Car drive_____
Neighborhood_____
Kids_____
Siblings_____
Parents_____
Other relatives_____
Friends_____
Favorite Music_____
Favorite Saying_____
Other_____
_____
_____

Character Description_____
_____
_____
_____
_____
Purpose in Story_____
_____
_____
_____
_____
Plots planned for Character_____
_____
_____
_____
_____

Sequel Setup/Cliffhangers_____
_____
_____
_____
Important Dates _____
_____
_____
Secrets _____
_____
_____
Character Key Points_____
_____
_____
_____

Additional Notes:

Character Profile

Name_____
Nick Name_____ Social Status _____
Age_____ Birthday_____
Height_____ Race _____ Sex_____
Weight_____ Religion_____

Body Type _____
_____
Body Assets (big butt, boobs,
muscular, basketball build, etc)_____
_____
_____
Personality_____
_____
_____
Dress style _____
_____
Other _____
_____
_____

Character Description_____
_____
_____
_____
Purpose in Story_____
_____
_____
_____
Plots planned for Character_____
_____
_____
_____

Lifestyle_____
Income class_____
House_____
Car drive_____
Neighborhood_____
Kids_____
Siblings_____
Parents_____
Other relatives_____
Friends_____
Favorite Music_____
Favorite Saying_____
Other_____
_____

Sequel Setup/Cliffhangers_____
_____
_____
Important Dates _____
_____
Secrets _____
_____
_____
Character Key Points_____
_____
_____
_____

Additional Notes:

Character Profile

Name_____
Nick Name_____ Social Status _____
Age_____ Birthday_____
Height_____ Race _____ Sex_____
Weight_____ Religion_____

Body Type _____

Body Assets (big butt, boobs, muscular, basketball build, etc)_____
_____
_____
_____

Personality_____
_____
_____

Dress style _____

Other _____
_____
_____

Lifestyle_____
Income class_____
House_____
Car drive_____
Neighborhood_____
Kids_____
Siblings_____
Parents_____
Other relatives_____
Friends_____
Favorite Music_____
Favorite Saying_____
Other_____
_____

Character Description_____
_____
_____
_____

Purpose in Story_____
_____
_____
_____

Plots planned for Character_____
_____
_____
_____
_____

Sequel Setup/Cliffhangers_____
_____
_____

Important Dates _____
_____

Secrets _____
_____
_____

Character Key Points_____
_____
_____

Additional Notes:

Character Profile

Name_____
Nick Name_____ Social Status _____
Age_____ Birthday_____
Height_____ Race _____ Sex_____
Weight_____ Religion

Body Type _____

Body Assets (big butt, boobs, muscular, basketball build, etc)_____
_____
_____
_____

Personality_____
_____
_____

Dress style _____

Other _____
_____
_____

Character Description_____
_____
_____
_____
_____

Purpose in Story_____
_____
_____
_____

Plots planned for Character_____
_____
_____
_____

Lifestyle_____
Income class_____
House_____
Car drive_____
Neighborhood_____
Kids_____
Siblings_____
Parents_____
Other relatives_____
Friends_____
Favorite Music_____
Favorite Saying_____
Other_____
_____
_____

Sequel Setup/Cliffhangers_____
_____
_____
_____

Important Dates _____
_____

Secrets _____
_____
_____

Character Key Points_____
_____
_____
_____

Additional Notes:

Character Profile

Name_____
Nick Name_____ Social Status _____
Age_____ Birthday_____
Height_____ Race _____Sex_____
Weight_____ Religion_____

Body Type _____

Body Assets (big butt, boobs, muscular, basketball build, etc)_____
_____
_____
_____

Personality_____
_____
_____

Dress style _____

Other _____
_____
_____

Lifestyle_____
Income class_____
House_____
Car drive_____
Neighborhood_____
Kids_____
Siblings_____
Parents_____
Other relatives_____
Friends_____
Favorite Music_____
Favorite Saying_____
Other_____
_____
_____

Character Description_____
_____
_____
_____
_____

Purpose in Story_____
_____
_____
_____

Plots planned for Character_____
_____
_____
_____

Sequel Setup/Cliffhangers_____
_____
_____

Important Dates _____
_____

Secrets _____
_____

Character Key Points_____
_____
_____
_____

Additional Notes:

Character Profile

Name_____
Nick Name_____ Social Status _____
Age_____ Birthday_____
Height_____ Race _____Sex_____
Weight_____ Religion_____

Body Type _____
_____
Body Assets (big butt, boobs,
muscular, basketball build, etc)_____
_____
_____
_____
Personality_____
_____
_____
Dress style _____
_____
Other _____
_____
_____
_____

Character Description_____
_____
_____
_____
_____
Purpose in Story_____
_____
_____
_____
_____
Plots planned for Character_____
_____
_____
_____
_____
_____

Lifestyle_____
Income class_____
House_____
Car drive_____
Neighborhood_____
Kids_____
Siblings_____
Parents_____
Other relatives_____
Friends_____
Favorite Music_____
Favorite Saying_____
Other_____
_____
_____

Sequel Setup/Cliffhangers_____
_____
_____
_____
Important Dates _____
_____
_____
Secrets _____
_____
_____
_____
Character Key Points_____
_____
_____
_____
_____

Additional Notes:

Character Profile

Name _____
Nick Name _____ Social Status _____
Age _____ Birthday _____
Height _____ Race _____ Sex _____
Weight _____ Religion

Body Type _____
Body Assets (big butt, boobs, muscular, basketball build, etc) _____
_____
_____
_____
Personality _____
_____
_____
Dress style _____
Other _____
_____
_____

Lifestyle _____
Income class _____
House _____
Car drive _____
Neighborhood _____
Kids _____
Siblings _____
Parents _____
Other relatives _____
Friends _____
Favorite Music _____
Favorite Saying _____
Other _____
_____

Character Description _____
_____
_____
_____
_____
Purpose in Story _____
_____
_____
_____
Plots planned for Character _____
_____
_____
_____

Sequel Setup/Cliffhangers _____
_____
_____
Important Dates _____
_____
Secrets _____
_____
_____
Character Key Points _____
_____
_____
_____

Additional Notes:

Character Profile

Name_____
Nick Name_____ Social Status _____
Age_____ Birthday_____
Height_____ Race _____ Sex _____
Weight_____ Religion_____

Body Type _____
_____
Body Assets (big butt, boobs,
muscular, basketball build, etc)_____
_____
_____
_____
Personality_____
_____
_____
Dress style _____
_____
Other _____
_____
_____
_____

Character Description_____
_____
_____
_____
Purpose in Story_____
_____
_____
_____
Plots planned for Character_____
_____
_____
_____
_____

Lifestyle_____
Income class_____
House_____
Car drive_____
Neighborhood_____
Kids_____
Siblings_____
Parents_____
Other relatives_____
Friends_____
Favorite Music_____
Favorite Saying_____
Other_____
_____
_____

Sequel Setup/Cliffhangers_____
_____
_____
_____
Important Dates _____
_____
Secrets _____
_____
_____
Character Key Points_____
_____
_____
_____

Additional Notes:

Character Relationships

Main Character

_____

Family Members

_____
_____
_____
_____
_____

Love Interest

_____
_____
_____
_____

Business Relationships

_____
_____
_____
_____

Other Character Relationships

_____
_____
_____
_____

Main Character

_____

Family Members

_____
_____
_____
_____
_____

Love Interest

_____
_____
_____
_____

Business Relationships

_____
_____
_____
_____

Other Character Relationships

_____
_____
_____
_____

Character Relationships

Main Character

_____

Family Members

_____
_____
_____
_____
_____

Love Interest

_____
_____
_____
_____

Business Relationships

_____
_____
_____
_____

Other Character Relationships

_____
_____
_____
_____
_____

Main Character

_____

Family Members

_____
_____
_____
_____
_____

Love Interest

_____
_____
_____
_____

Business Relationships

_____
_____
_____
_____

Other Character Relationships

_____
_____
_____
_____
_____

Character Relationships

Main Character | Main Character

_____ | _____

Family Members | Family Members

_____ | _____
_____ | _____
_____ | _____
_____ | _____
_____ | _____
_____ | _____

Love Interest | Love Interest

_____ | _____
_____ | _____
_____ | _____

Business Relationships | Business Relationships

_____ | _____
_____ | _____
_____ | _____

Other Character Relationships | Other Character Relationships

_____ | _____
_____ | _____
_____ | _____
_____ | _____

Character Relationships

Main Character

_____

Family Members

_____
_____
_____
_____
_____

Love Interest

_____
_____
_____

Business Relationships

_____
_____
_____

Other Character Relationships

_____
_____
_____
_____

Main Character

_____

Family Members

_____
_____
_____
_____
_____

Love Interest

_____
_____
_____

Business Relationships

_____
_____
_____

Other Character Relationships

_____
_____
_____
_____

Sub-Character Quick Snapshot

***Name _____ Nickname _____
Age _____ Gender _____ Height _____ Race _____
Characteristics _____
Character relations _____
Purpose in story _____
_____
_____
_____

***Name _____ Nickname _____
Age _____ Gender _____ Height _____ Race _____
Characteristics _____
Character relations _____
Purpose in story _____
_____
_____
_____

***Name _____ Nickname _____
Age _____ Gender _____ Height _____ Race _____
Characteristics _____
Character relations _____
Purpose in story _____
_____
_____
_____

***Name _____ Nickname _____
Age _____ Gender _____ Height _____ Race _____
Characteristics _____
Character relations _____
Purpose in story _____
_____
_____
_____

***Name _____ Nickname _____
Age _____ Gender _____ Height _____ Race _____
Characteristics _____
Character relations _____
Purpose in story _____
_____
_____
_____

Sub-Character Quick Snapshot

***Name _____ Nickname _____
Age _____ Gender _____ Height _____ Race _____
Characteristics_____
Character relations _____
Purpose in story_____
_____
_____
_____

***Name _____ Nickname _____
Age _____ Gender _____ Height _____ Race _____
Characteristics_____
Character relations _____
Purpose in story_____
_____
_____
_____

***Name _____ Nickname _____
Age _____ Gender _____ Height _____ Race _____
Characteristics_____
Character relations _____
Purpose in story_____
_____
_____
_____

***Name _____ Nickname _____
Age _____ Gender _____ Height _____ Race _____
Characteristics_____
Character relations _____
Purpose in story_____
_____
_____
_____

***Name _____ Nickname _____
Age _____ Gender _____ Height _____ Race _____
Characteristics_____
Character relations _____
Purpose in story_____
_____
_____
_____

Character Table of Content

Name	Character Description

Time Capsule

The time capsule is your map of events that take place at a certain time in your story.

For instance, if someone is pregnant in your story you want to know at what point in the story did she get pregnant, how far along will she be when this happens or that happens and what date/time will she be expected to deliver her baby.

When did someone cheat? On what day is the release party? If you are talking about a murder, are you giving your characters alibi's? What is the exact time of the murder? What time frame is the alibi?

What day is a chapter written if it is a reflection in time? Are you writing your book in the summer, then winter months? What will your characters wear when it is cold outside? You wouldn't want to have them in shorts and sandals and its freezing outside in that state at Thanksgiving time. Do you even mention holidays?

You must know your timing of events in your story as you are writing so that everything you are talking about make sense in its own perfect timing. You don't want your character getting pregnant in June and having her baby in July. That simply does not make sense and is not realistic.

Use this space to write out your time capsule of events that take place throughout your story. Only concentrate on timing here and list the time related details. You will be surprised at how often you will need to reference this section as you are writing your amazing story!

Time Capsule

List the sequence of events that take place in the story.

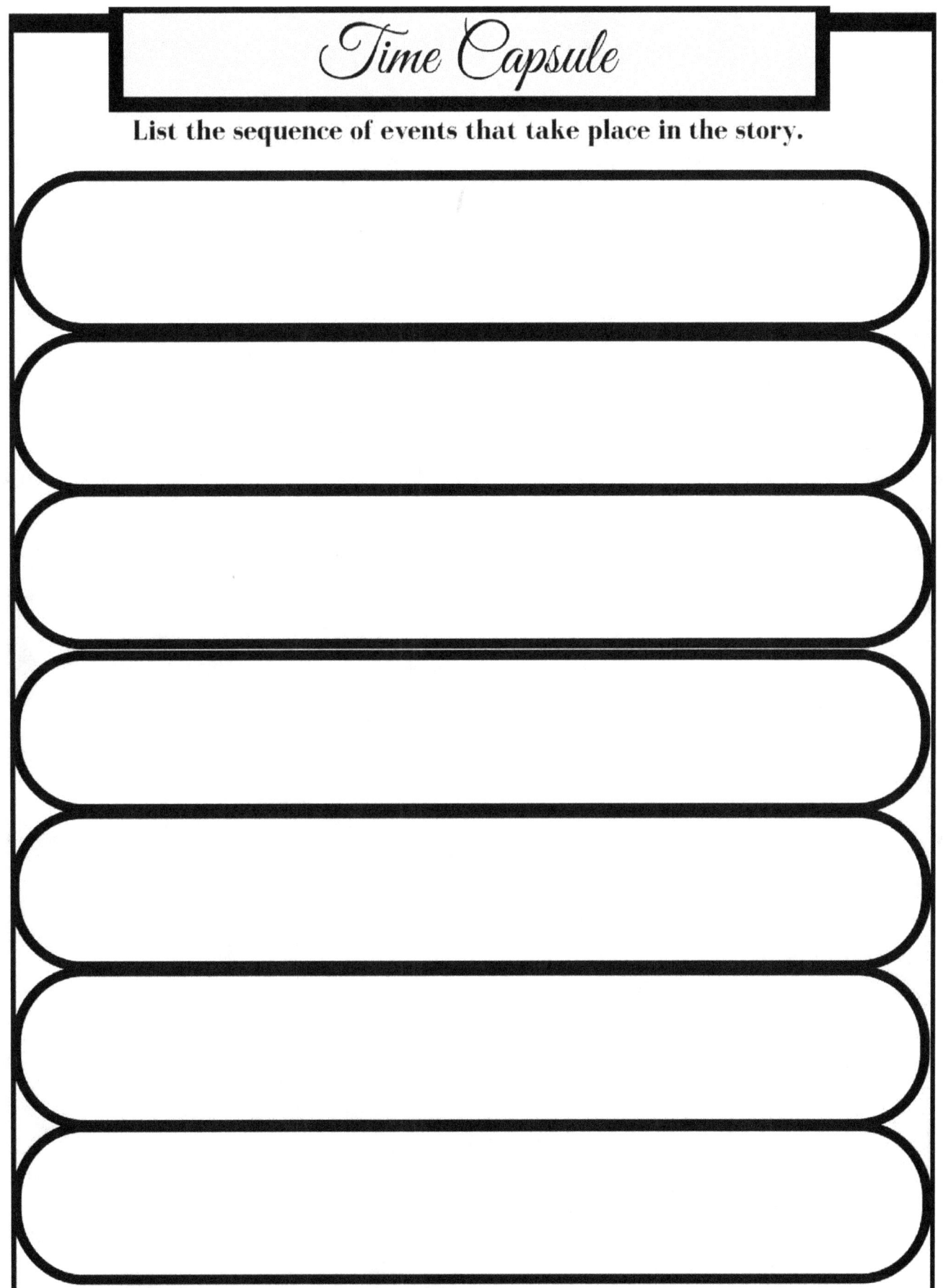

Time Capsule

List the sequence of events that take place in the story.

Time Capsule

List the sequence of events that take place in the story.

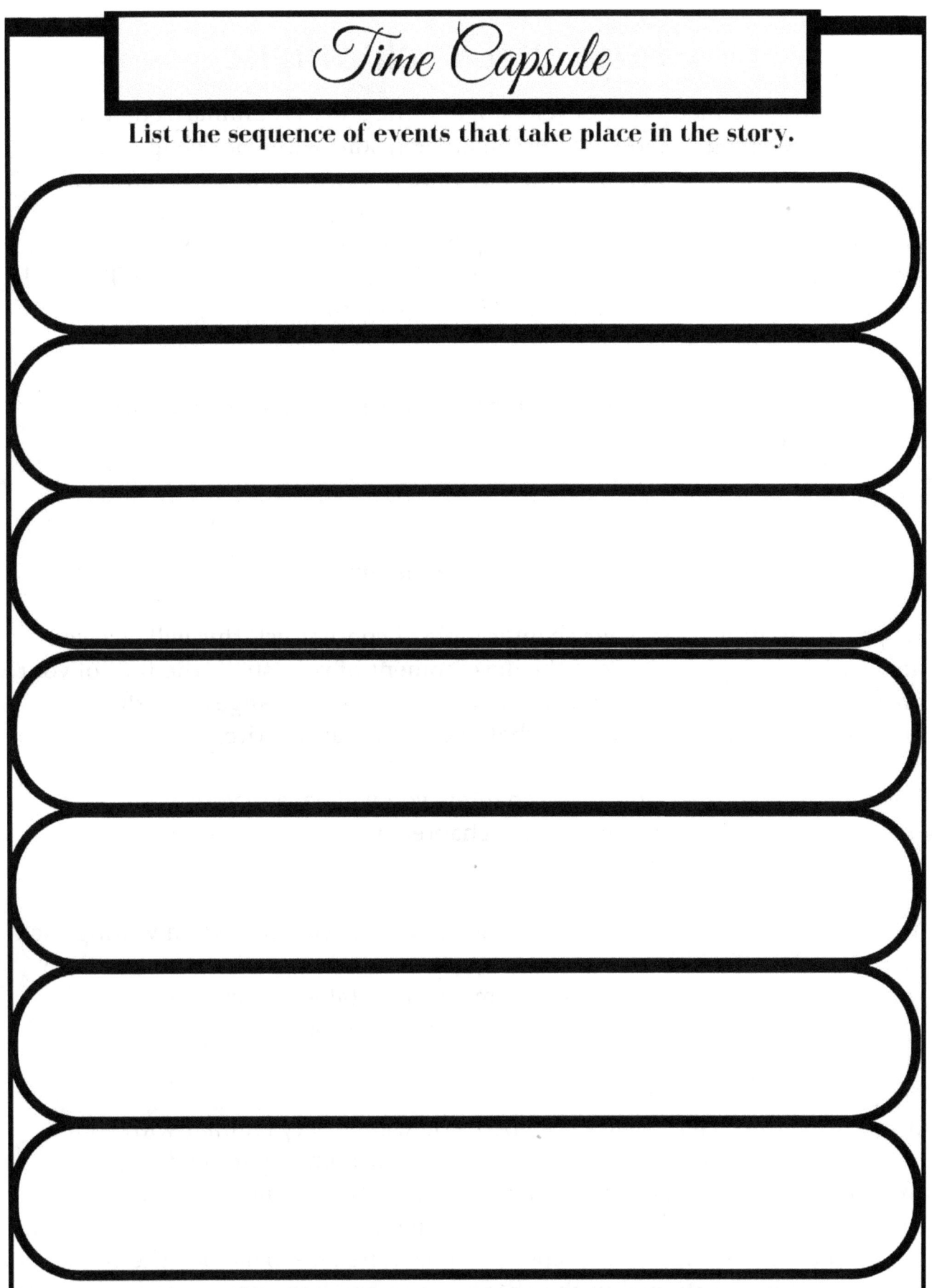

Chapter Development

Now that the characters are developed, and the story is summarized, it is time to start developing chapters in the book. First, start with your chapter table of contents. Write a few words or a sentence to sum up what that chapter is about. You want to be brief but give yourself enough to know what that chapter is and should be about. Seeing this snapshot of chapters will give you an idea on sequence of chapters to ensure they flow and make sense. This will be a chance to move chapters around if you need to.

Example:
Chapter 1 - Bryson Mathews starts his homeless journey at the park where he meets Brielle and her children.

Chapter 2 - Main Character is shot

Chapter 3 - Christmas Day Chaos, Proposal happens

As you are writing down your chapter table of content list, this will give you another opportunity to look at the development of your story, the flow of your chapters, the sequence of events, and make necessary changes as well as become even more familiar with what you are about to write.

You will be able to see how many chapters you will have in your book, if you need to split any chapters or add to a chapter. This will also be your opportunity to see if you should add any additional chapters or delete a few.

Your chapter table of content will be used as your reference when writing each chapter. When I complete my outlining process, every portion of my outline serves a very important purpose, but my chapter table of contents and my chapter summary are probably the most important piece when writing my story.

By the time the chapters are developed, you will be very familiar with your characters, your ideas for your story and any key points that need to be mentioned. You will also know what your plots, twists, and any events that need to happen and when they need to happen.
When you start to write your chapter summary, be sure to include the characters that should be mentioned in the chapter, and any important details about the

chapter. When you go back to read the summary, or if anyone else goes back to read the summary, you, or they, should know what the chapter should be about and how it should be written. Although, no two people would write a chapter the same, with a blueprint on what to write, both should be able to write the chapter with similarities if you have written a good chapter summary.

Example:

Chapter 6 - Bryson Mathews picked up his fiancée Jewel's buzzing phone that was left on the kitchen counter to silence it, only to realize she had a flirtatious text message flashing across her screen from a saved name that said, "boo thang." The message led him to call his best friend Kenneth to talk about it and also his investigator Mike to see if he could find out if she was cheating. What he found was shocking and so heart breaking for Bryson. He then set her up to catch her in the act, letting her know they were not be getting married. That day their relationship ended before it had a chance to start.

Chapter 15 - Jewel corners Brielle at Bryson's office as she enters with a picnic basket full of lunch she prepared for her and Bryson. Jewel tells her she is marrying Bryson and he was using her for a project. When she was shown a video of them together she didn't know what to believe. As Bryson was coming down the elevator he saw Brielle with tears in her eyes as she ran out of the building. When he saw Jewel smiling he feared the worse.

Write good chapter summaries and a good chapter table of content so that when you start to write your book, you will know exactly what that story should sound like, look like, and feel like. Write it just like you would speak it if you were talking to your friend. You got this, and I am sure your story will be amazing!

Chapter Table of Content

1.
2.
3.
4.
5.
6.
7.
8.
9.
10.
11.
12.
13.
14.
15.

Chapter Table of Content

16. _____
17. _____
18. _____
19. _____
20. _____
21. _____
22. _____
23. _____
24. _____
25. _____
26. _____
27. _____
28. _____
29. _____
30. _____

Chapter Table of Content

31. _____
_____
32. _____
_____
33. _____
_____
34. _____
_____
35. _____
_____
36. _____
_____
37. _____
_____
38. _____
_____
39. _____
_____
40. _____
_____
41. _____
_____
42. _____
_____
43. _____
_____
44. _____
_____
45. _____

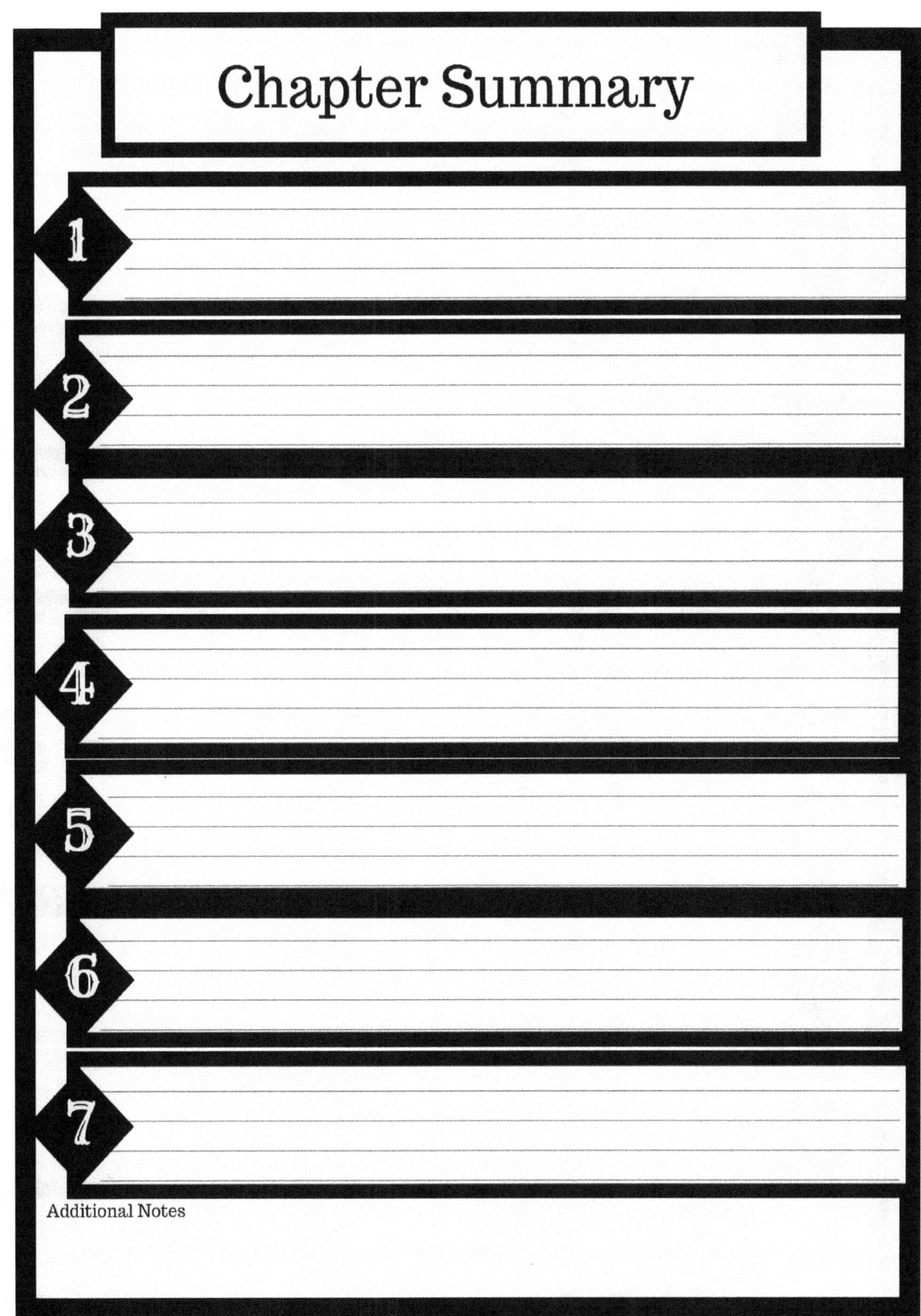

Chapter Summary

8

9

10

11

12

13

14

Additional Notes

Chapter Summary

15

16

17

18

19

20

21

Additional

Chapter Summary

22

23

24

25

26

27

28

Additional

Chapter Summary

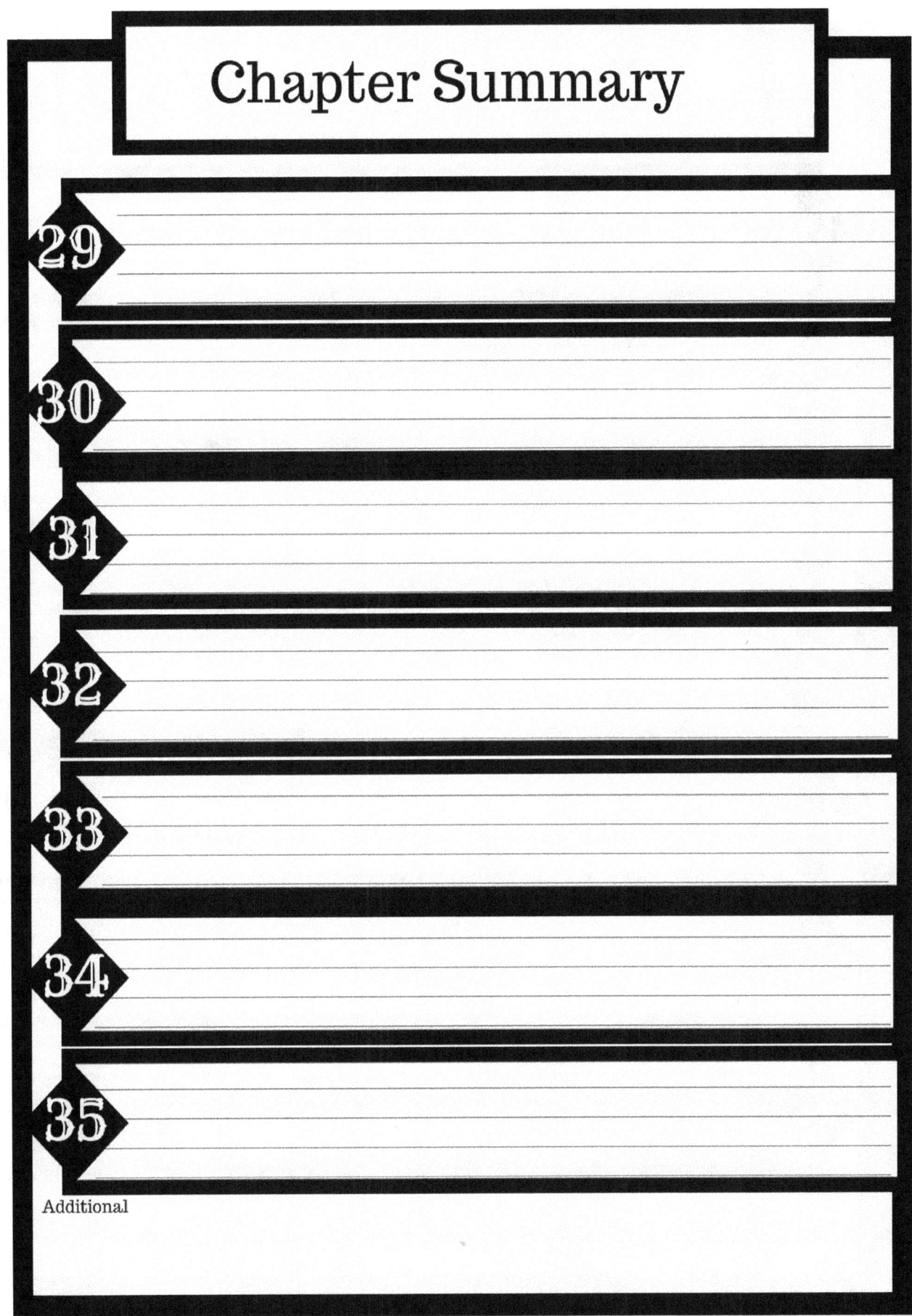

Additional

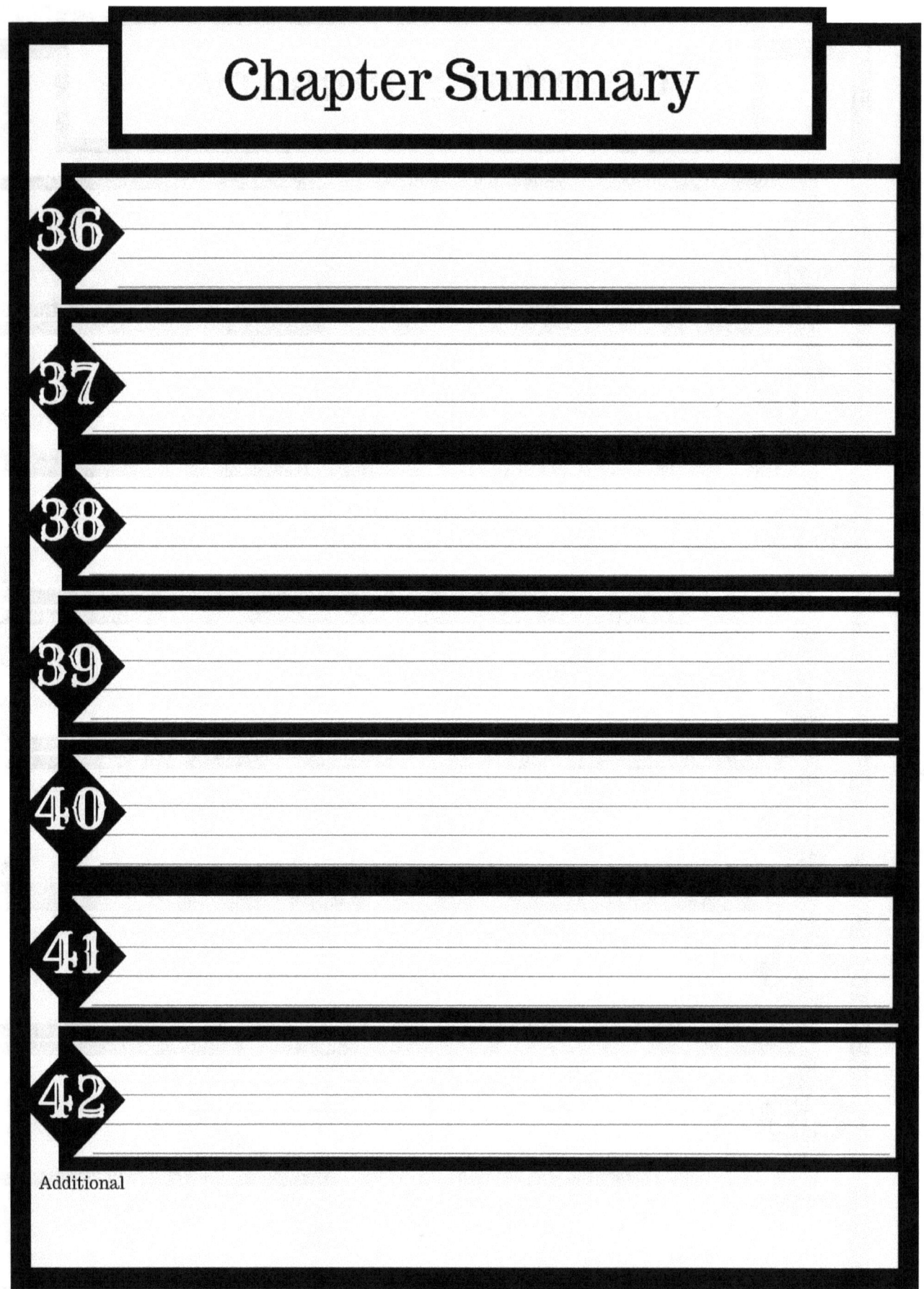

Chapter Summary

- 36
- 37
- 38
- 39
- 40
- 41
- 42

Additional

Plot Development

This section should be fun for you as you develop your plots. Use this section to identify what your plots are specifically and how you will develop and plan them out with every chapter written in your story.

Identify what the plot is specifically, then start to develop your plot by knowing what you want to happen and how you want it to happen. Figure out when the plot will start to develop in your story and when you want to reveal your ah ha moment. What twist and turns will be involved with each plot? What characters are affected with each plot. What events need to happen that will lead up to the complete development of the plot.

Every story should have plots to make it interesting and keep your readers interested in what they are reading. Your story should keep your readers wanting to read more page after page. Imagine reading a book with no storyline, no plot, just a never-ending story that had no punch line or nothing to look forward to at the end. Would you want to keep reading? What will make you keep picking that book up? Don't write that book.

You don't want your books to drag on and on. What you want is for people to think of your book(s) you write as a page turner. A book that keeps the readers interest, a book that has something for readers to look forward to page after page, because they need to know what is happening next. This is why books have plots. Write and develop great plots and give your readers something to look forward to. Write that page turner that is full of great interesting plots.

Who Killed Bill? Did he find out she was cheating on him? Does he get the girl even though her mind was tainted with lies? Who is the baby daddy? Who was shot? Did she ever find the girl under the bed? He is about to get married, when is he going to find out his best friend slept with his girl? Keep them wondering what will happen next, how will the book end.

Whatever the plot is for your story develop it and make it good. You can have several plots within your story, you choose how many to make your story flow and interesting, to make your story a page turner! What you write is up to you, just make it amazing!

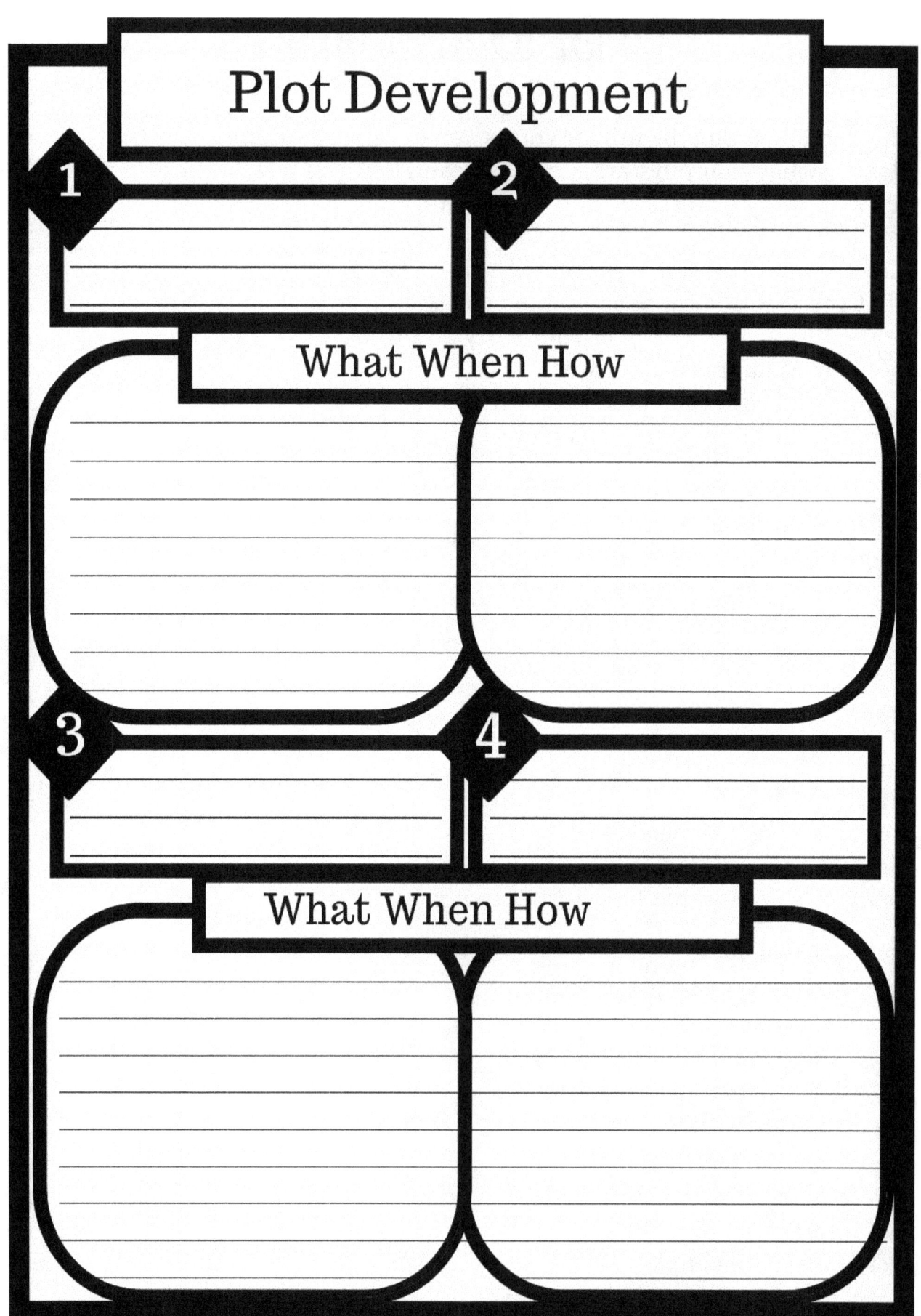

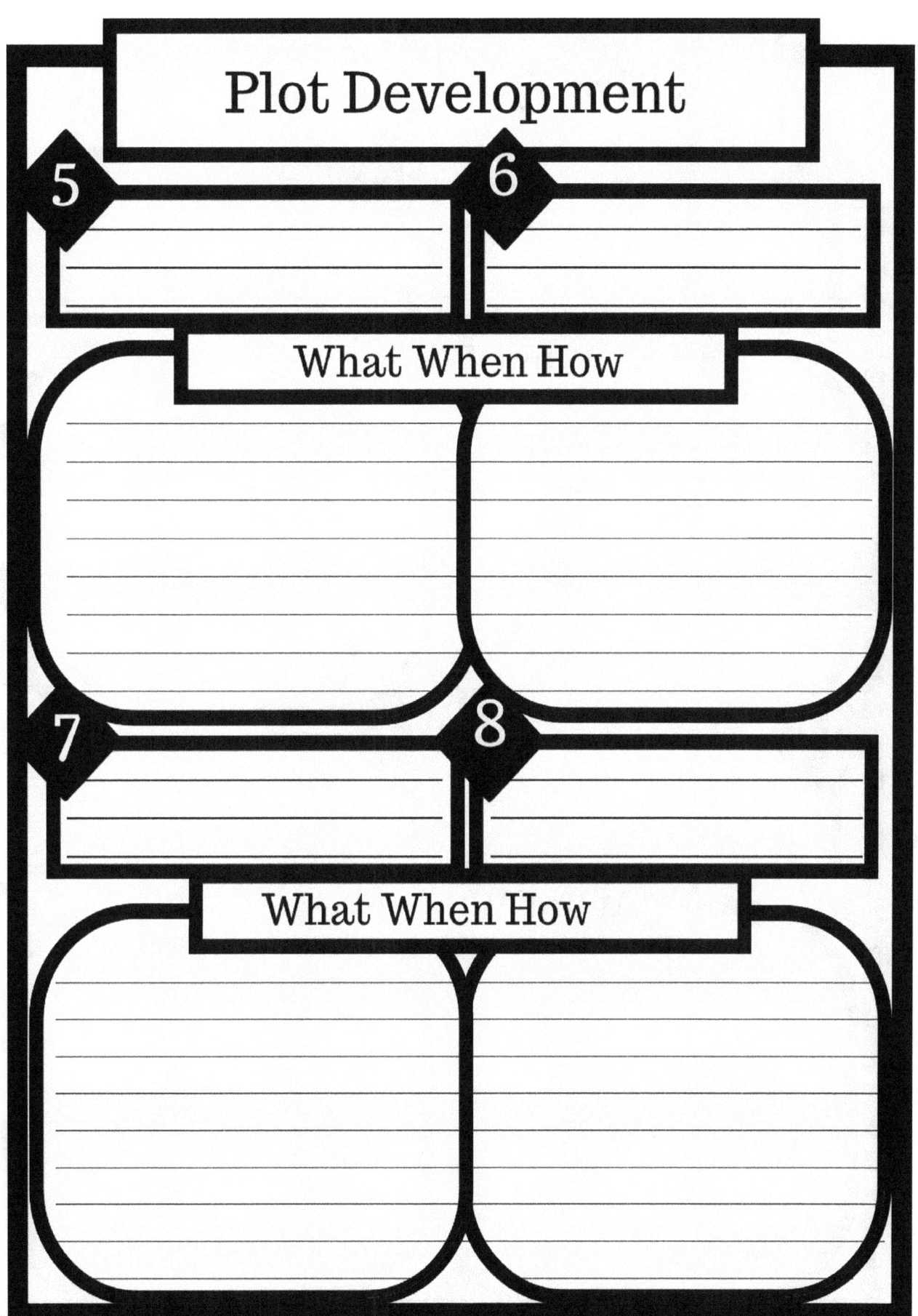

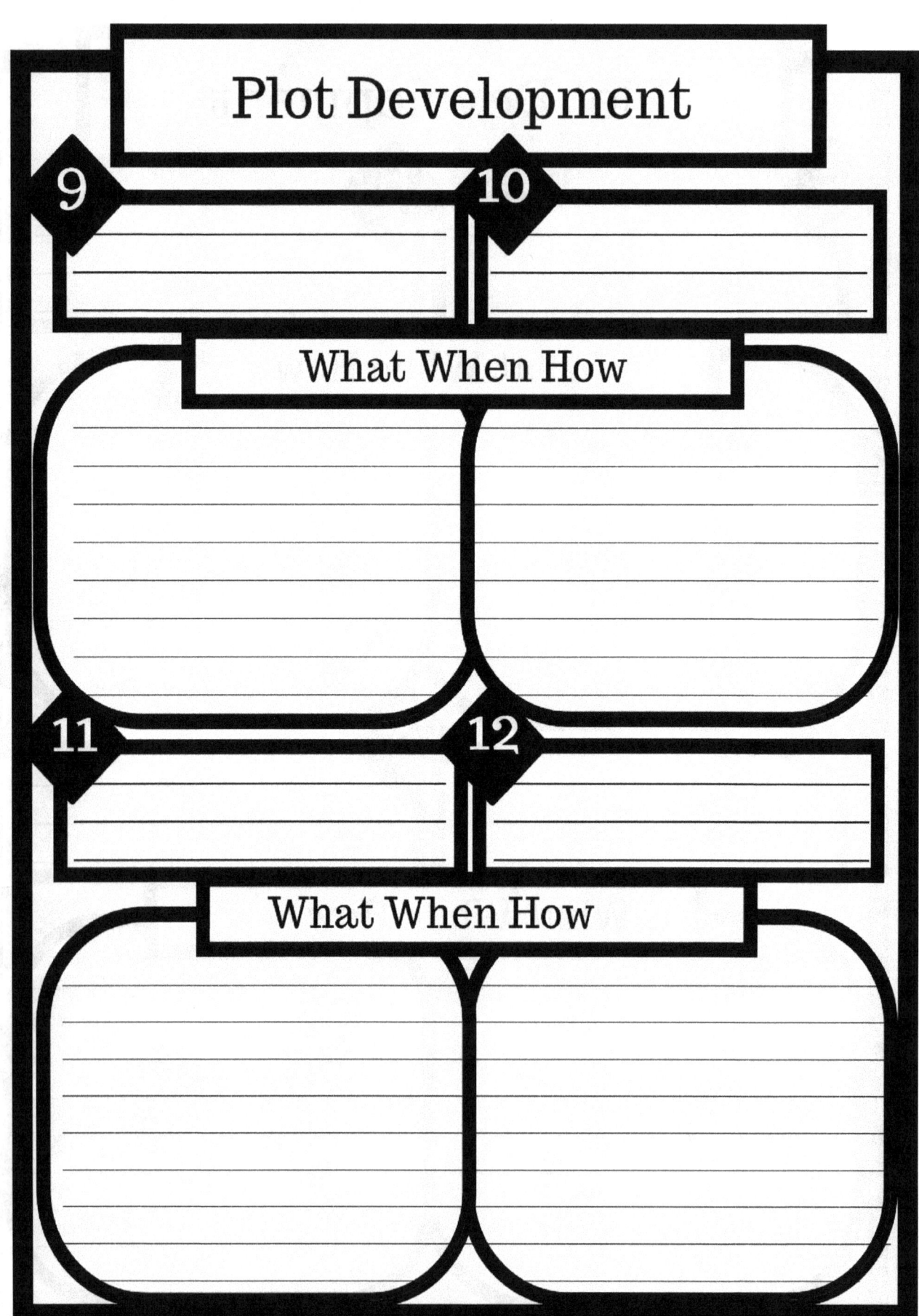

Scene/Setting Development

Now, here we are thinking about the scene, the setting in which the chapter will take place. When writing your book, each chapter will be set in some building or not, at some time of the day, day or night. It will feel some type of way, smell some type of way, and look some type of way. You want to paint a picture for your readers, make them feel what you feel, smell what you smell, and see what you see.

Use the space provided to develop your scenes. Start painting the picture you want your readers to read. When you imagine how your story will play out, you also visualize a place, a color, a descriptive scene. Write what you see in your imagination, what you visualize just as you want your readers to visualize. Now it is a given that every reader will visualize what you write, but in their own way. You just build the concept of what it should look like, paint the picture of your scene as you see it to be to help them see what you see.

They met at a diner in the middle of the desert. It was small and crowded with only a dozen people inside. But the coziness of the small dusty red building with four tables and a six-foot bar, gave them comfort in the middle of the desert, where snakes and ugly, jumping, black and brown, golf ball size critters came from out of nowhere. They were stranded in no-man's land without a car, or another building in sight. It was a hundred and ten degrees, hot and stuffy in the dry desert heat as they waited for someone to come rescue them from what seemed like a death trap.

This was an example, but I am sure you visualized the diner, the people, the desert, the snakes and the ugly critters from your perspective. Develop your scenes, and as you write, add more to what you want your readers to see from your painting of words on the page.

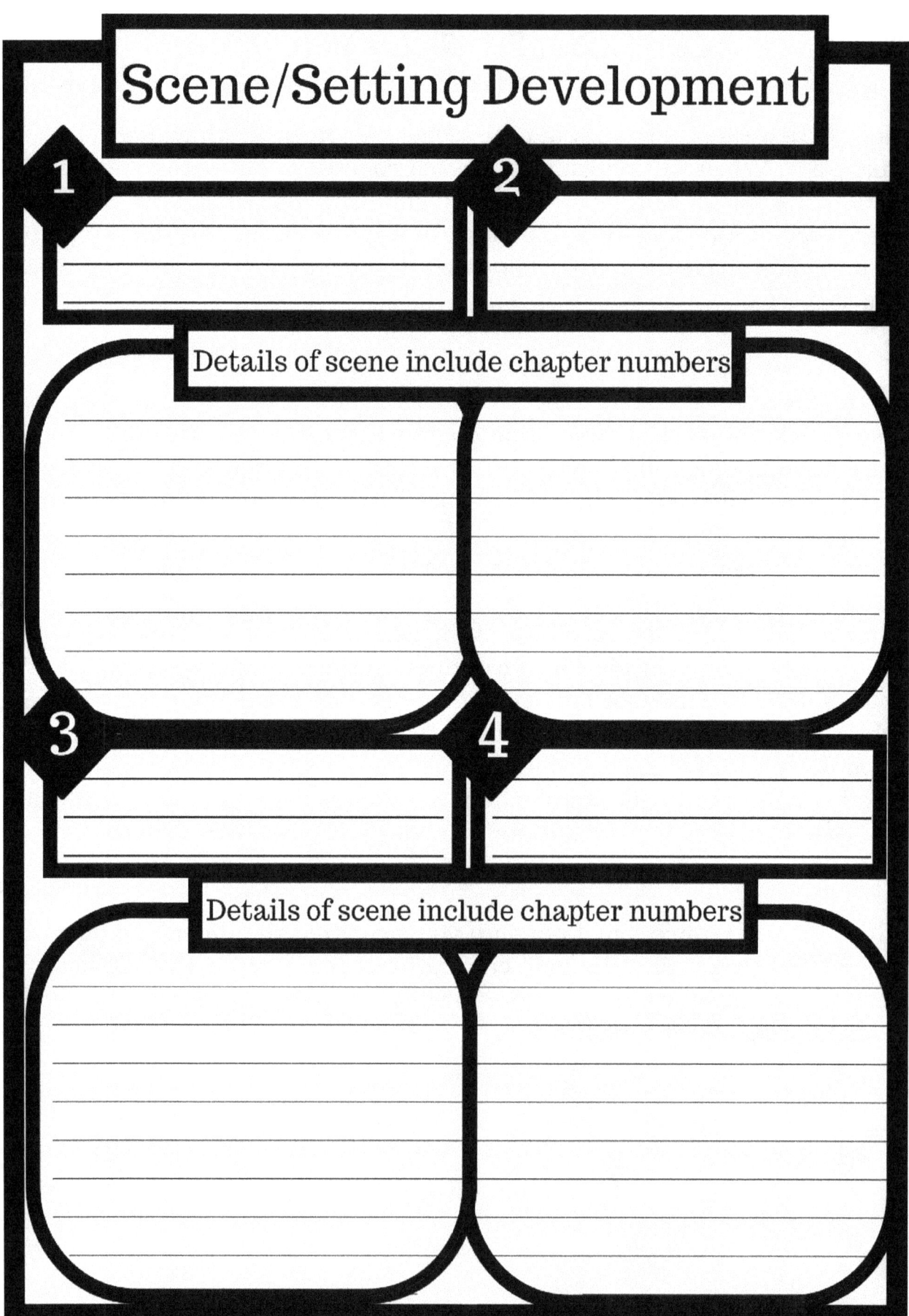

Scene/Setting Development

5.

6.

Details of scene include chapter numbers

7.

8.

Details of scene include chapter numbers

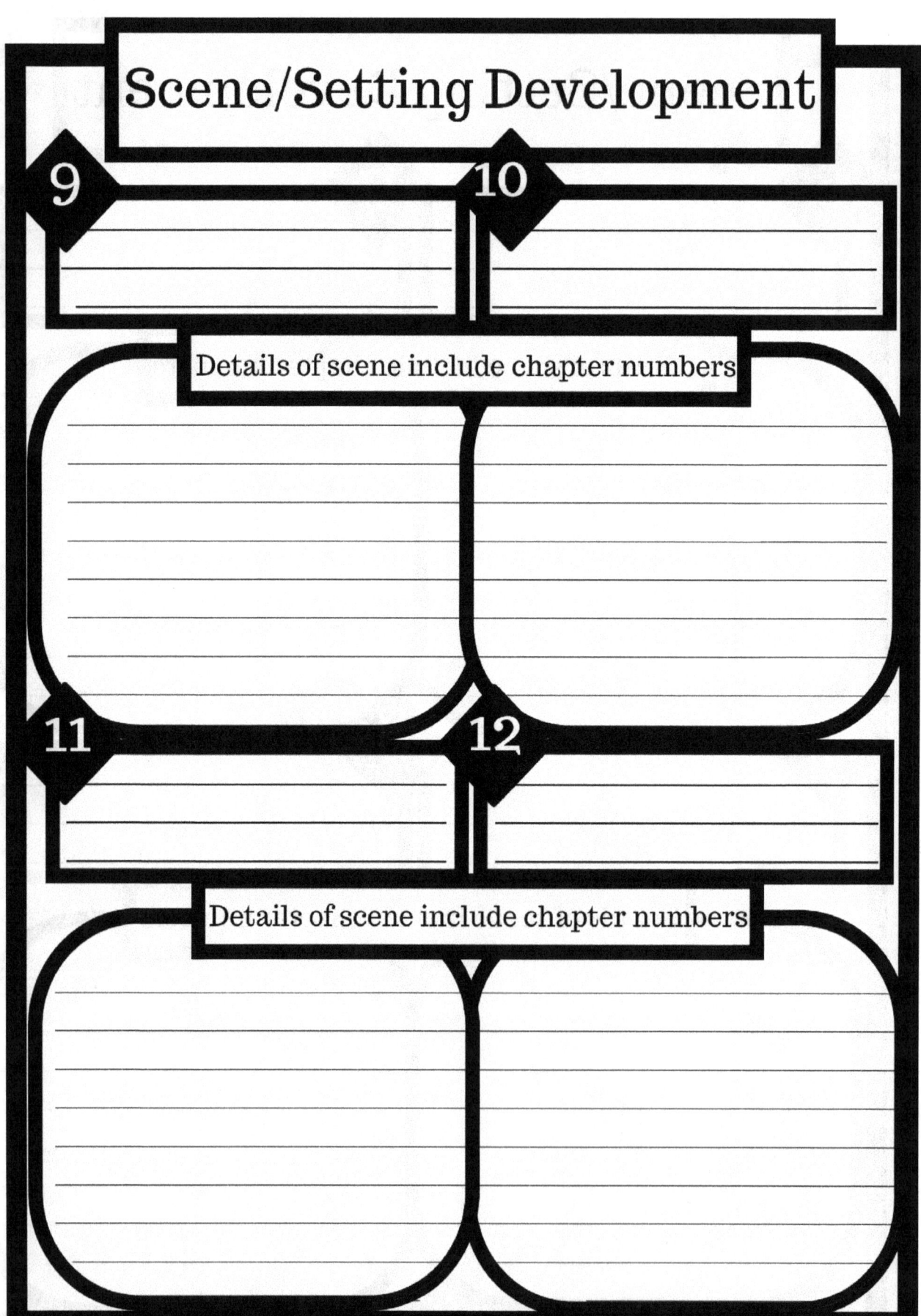

Scene/Setting Development

13.

14.

Details of scene include chapter numbers

15.

16.

Details of scene include chapter numbers

Writing First Chapter

First chapters are very important and require thought and a plan to ensure it is written well and written with the intention to lure your readers into your book.

When writing your first chapter you want to make sure that when readers pick up your book and start reading the first few pages, they will be hooked. From the first paragraph you want your readers to want more, to not want to put your book down because it is just that good, it intrigues them and makes them desire more. It should capture their attention to where they must know what happens next and must know how the story ends. Your first chapter should be an attention grabber! It should start to introduce your main characters and let the readers know what characters they will be falling in love with or hate. Give them an idea of what drama, romance, scandal, mystery, etc. they can anticipate as they read your story. The goal is to make sure you write an attention grabbing first chapter!

When introducing your characters in the first chapter you should give your readers a sense of who they are and what they are about without giving away too much of your story resolution. You want them to start getting to know your characters and be able to feel like they know them but still need to "get to know them." As the story continues, so will your character development. But introducing your characters early on in the beginning chapters is very important. The readers will know who the story is about and will not be confused if you introduce a main character later on in your story. Although, it is ok to introduce supporting characters later in your story, it's not a good idea to introduce main characters late. The "later" added supporting characters could become main characters in a sequel if you plan to write a sequel to your story.

Your first chapter should introduce a plot or two or give a clue of a plot unveiling. If someone dies in your first chapter, one plot could be who killed them or how did they really die? Or how a loved one, wife/husband was able to cope and move on, did they find love again? Did the best friend who really had a thing for her friends' spouse pursue him at their weakest moment grieving? Did a pregnancy happen after a night of forbidden passion? Maybe the ending of the story was briefly mentioned, and it was the main plot of the story but to find out how that plot develops you are able to write other plots that lead up to the reveal. The first chapter is the setup to the rest of your story and your readers will need a great start that they want more of. Spend time thinking about your first chapter and how you will make it amazing to capture your readers attention.

Writing First Chapter

First Chapter Characters _____
_____
_____
_____
_____
_____
_____
_____

First Chapter Attention Grabber Scenes _____
_____
_____
_____
_____
_____
_____
_____

First Chapter Plot Introduction Setup _____
_____
_____
_____
_____
_____
_____
_____
_____
_____

First Chapter Notes _____
_____
_____
_____
_____
_____
_____
_____

Sequel Setup

Setting up a sequel happens way before you get to the ending of the book. Think about watching your favorite sitcom episode. When the thirty-minute to hour show ends, there is a stopping point, and a really good sitcom will end with a setup to be continued with the next episode. If you are anything like me, you can't wait until the next episode airs, so you can see what happens next. Same concept when writing a book. You want your readers to want to know what happens next with each chapter but also with the sequel, your next book.

When your readers get to the end of your book, you want them to feel fulfilled, but you also want them to patiently and anxiously anticipate the next book coming out. Set up your story to be an amazing read chapter after chapter, and when you get to the end of the book, end it with a hanging plot, a cliffhanger that leaves your readers feeling fulfilled but at the same time leaves them anticipating the next book.

Plan your sequel before you get to the end of your story. Start thinking about what will happen that will setup the sequel. When I ended "Love Never Fails," the scandalous cheating Jewel was pregnant, leaving everyone guessing who the father of her baby was. Could it be the man she cheated on her fiancé with, or his brother she seduced and blackmailed saying she would scream rape? So much went on in the story around all three characters that if she was pregnant by any one of them it would bring drama to their lives. That was the biggest "what happened next" setup but there were so many other un-answered questions that made readers anticipate the next book.

Think about an amazing sequel setup and write an amazing story developing the setup throughout the chapters so when you get to the end, your readers will say how great of a story teller you are and how they can't wait for the next book to read more. Setup your sequel, and leave your readers wanting more!

Sequel Setup

Sequel Idea _____
_____
_____
_____
_____
_____
_____

Sequel Plots, Twist & Turns _____
_____
_____
_____
_____
_____
_____

Sequel Setup _____
_____
_____
_____
_____
_____
_____
_____
_____
_____
_____
_____

Sequel Notes _____
_____
_____
_____
_____
_____

27 Day Writing Plan

**Write for 27 Days, no days off, 2,250 word count a day for average 60,000 word count final word count total would be 60,750.

**Write 5 days during weekday, off 2 days on weekends, total writing days = 20, total off days = 7, write 3,000 words a day for average 60,000 word count final word count would be 60,000.

**Write 4 days a week, off 3 days a week, total writing days = 16, total off days = 11, write 3,750 words a day for average 60,000 word count final word count would be 60,000.

**Write 3 days a week, off 4 days a week, total writing days = 12, total off days = 15, write 5000 words a day for average 60,000 word count final word count would be 60,000.

** You choose what works best for you, plan it, and stick to your plan!

27 Day Writing Plan

When planning your 27-day writing plan you want to be realistic in setting writing goals. Previously you should have figured out how many days you have in a week to write and what days you would set aside to dedicate to the writing of your book. You should already have a writing space where you won't be disturbed, and you should already know how long you will have to write. So, planning your writing should be easy.

Figure out your daily word count, this will be determined by how fast or slow you type. Since you have a well written outlined writing plan, you should be able to flow with your writing because you already know what you are going to write and how you will write it. Every piece of your book is already planned out, so writers block should not exist. Typing at a steady pace should be easy, figuring out your hourly and daily word count should be easy.

As you start to write, if you are going over your daily word count then that is a bonus. If you are not meeting your daily goal, that's ok too. Take note of what you lack and make it up on another day. As you write and become engaged in your story you may find yourself writing and not wanting to stop. Just start writing and adjust your writing schedule as needed. Most important thing to remember is to keep writing. Dedication and consistency is the key to completing your book! So, plan your commitment and be committed to your plan.

27 Day Writing Plan

Day 1
Day 2
Day 3
Day 4

Day 5
Day 6
Day 7
Day 8
Day 9
Day 10
Day 11

Day 12
Day 13
Day 14
Day 15
Day 16
Day 17
Day 18
Day 19

Day 20
Day 21
Day 22
Day 23
Day 24
Day 25
Day 26
Day 27

After Completing 27 Day Writing Challenge whats left?
*
*
*
*
*
*
*

Additional Notes:

27 Day Writing Plan

Day 1
Day 2
Day 3
Day 4

Day 5
Day 6
Day 7
Day 8
Day 9
Day 10
Day 11

Day 12
Day 13
Day 14
Day 15
Day 16
Day 17
Day 18
Day 19

Day 20
Day 21
Day 22
Day 23
Day 24
Day 25
Day 26
Day 27

After Completing 27 Day Writing Challenge whats left?
*
*
*
*
*
*
*

Additional Notes:

Daily Word Count

In the space provided here, keep up with your daily word count. This will help you stay on track with your writing goals. If you have word count unmet then be sure to make-up for those words on another day.

01
Daily Word Goal

Beginning Word Count

Ending Word Count

Total Word Goal Met

Total Word Goal Un-Met

02
Daily Word Goal

Beginning Word Count

Ending Word Count

Total Word Goal Met

Total Word Goal Un-Met

03
Daily Word Goal

Beginning Word Count

Ending Word Count

Total Word Goal Met

Total Word Goal Un-Met

04
Daily Word Goal

Beginning Word Count

Ending Word Count

Total Word Goal Met

Total Word Goal Un-Met

05
Daily Word Goal

Beginning Word Count

Ending Word Count

Total Word Goal Met

Total Word Goal Un-Met

06
Daily Word Goal

Beginning Word Count

Ending Word Count

Total Word Goal Met

Total Word Goal Un-Met

Week _____ of _____ Completed ___

07
Total Weekly Word Goal _____

Word Goal Met _____

Total Un-Met Word Goal _____

Make up Word Goal _____

Word Goal Met _____

01
Daily Word Goal

Beginning Word Count

Ending Word Count

Total Word Goal Met

Total Word Goal Un-Met

02
Daily Word Goal

Beginning Word Count

Ending Word Count

Total Word Goal Met

Total Word Goal Un-Met

03
Daily Word Goal

Beginning Word Count

Ending Word Count

Total Word Goal Met

Total Word Goal Un-Met

04
Daily Word Goal

Beginning Word Count

Ending Word Count

Total Word Goal Met

Total Word Goal Un-Met

05
Daily Word Goal

Beginning Word Count

Ending Word Count

Total Word Goal Met

Total Word Goal Un-Met

06
Daily Word Goal

Beginning Word Count

Ending Word Count

Total Word Goal Met

Total Word Goal Un-Met

Week _____ of _____ Completed _____

07
Total Weekly Word Goal _____
Word Goal Met _____
Total Un-Met Word Goal _____
Make up Word Goal _____
Word Goal Met _____

01
Daily Word Goal

Beginning Word Count

Ending Word Count

Total Word Goal Met

Total Word Goal Un-Met

02
Daily Word Goal

Beginning Word Count

Ending Word Count

Total Word Goal Met

Total Word Goal Un-Met

03
Daily Word Goal

Beginning Word Count

Ending Word Count

Total Word Goal Met

Total Word Goal Un-Met

04
Daily Word Goal

Beginning Word Count

Ending Word Count

Total Word Goal Met

Total Word Goal Un-Met

05
Daily Word Goal

Beginning Word Count

Ending Word Count

Total Word Goal Met

Total Word Goal Un-Met

06
Daily Word Goal

Beginning Word Count

Ending Word Count

Total Word Goal Met

Total Word Goal Un-Met

Week _____ *of* _____ *Completed* _____

07
Total Weekly Word Goal_____
Word Goal Met _____
Total Un-Met Word Goal_____
Make up Word Goal _____
Word Goal Met _____

01
Daily Word Goal

Beginning Word Count

Ending Word Count

Total Word Goal Met

Total Word Goal Un-Met

02
Daily Word Goal

Beginning Word Count

Ending Word Count

Total Word Goal Met

Total Word Goal Un-Met

03
Daily Word Goal

Beginning Word Count

Ending Word Count

Total Word Goal Met

Total Word Goal Un-Met

04
Daily Word Goal

Beginning Word Count

Ending Word Count

Total Word Goal Met

Total Word Goal Un-Met

05
Daily Word Goal

Beginning Word Count

Ending Word Count

Total Word Goal Met

Total Word Goal Un-Met

06
Daily Word Goal

Beginning Word Count

Ending Word Count

Total Word Goal Met

Total Word Goal Un-Met

Week _____ *of* _____ *Completed* _____

07
Total Weekly Word Goal _____
Word Goal Met _____
Total Un-Met Word Goal _____
Make up Word Goal _____
Word Goal Met _____

Writing Mood   ## *Music for Mood*

Mood _____ Music _____
_____ _____
_____ _____
_____ _____

Mood _____ Music _____
_____ _____
_____ _____
_____ _____

Mood _____ Music _____
_____ _____
_____ _____
_____ _____

Mood _____ Music _____
_____ _____
_____ _____
_____ _____

Mood _____ Music _____
_____ _____
_____ _____
_____ _____

Mood _____ Music _____
_____ _____
_____ _____
_____ _____

Mood _____ Music _____
_____ _____
_____ _____
_____ _____

Snack List

Healthy Snacks

Feel Good Snacks

Beverages

More Feel Good Snacks

To Do List/Checklist

[] Start thinking about your book cover design. Find someone who can design you an amazing eye-catching cover that anyone would be tempted to pick up when they see your book on the shelf.

[] Think about the size you want your book to be 5x7, 6x9, etc. you decide.

[] Create you a social media account for your book/author name. Start marketing yourself and your book as soon as possible

[] Start marketing your book at least 30 days prior to your release date. Social Media, marketing plan, family & friends.

[] Think about what your brand is for your book and start branding yourself as you promote your book.

[] Research your publishing options. Traditional versus Self-publishing, Major publishing house versus Print on Demand like Amazon Creatspace or Ingram Sparks.

[] Get you an accountability partner who can check on your status and keep you on track with your writing.

[] Create a budget for expenses you may incur like book cover, editing, marketing, books to have on hand.

[] Do, do, do, and do some more. Write, write, write, and write some more. Yes you can!

[] Believe in yourself!

Frequently Asked Questions

How do you prevent writers block?

Writer's block is just a poor writers plan. When people outline first, plan their writing blueprint before they start the writing process, saying they have writers block should never exist. Because each character, each chapter, the scenes, the plots and the entire story development has been planned out and all you have to do is follow the blueprint to write and complete your book. Writers block will not exist.

What is the best way to get started writing a book?

When I am asked this question I always say by outlining. I live by this method, I use this method with every book I write or have an idea for. This is how I teach clients how to write and pull their ideas from thought to completed book. I always advise them to start by writing down all of their ideas and summarize their story as best as they can until they are ready to outline. With the right mindset and the right plan (Writing Blueprint) anyone can get started writing a book.

When should I start to worry about editing?

After you complete the book is when you will need to have your book edited. Finding a professional editor to edit your book is important to making your already amazing story better. Some people who try to cut cost may find a few people around them to read and edit their book before publishing and then compile all the corrections to fix themselves. But keep in mind that some needed corrections may be missed if you decide to take a shortcut on editing to save money. Write your book and then start the editing process.

How often should I re-read my story as I write?

In the past I would read as I write, so much so that I couldn't write the book because I was always reading. So I figured out a method that worked. I would write a chapter, then read only that chapter and move on to write the next. I wouldn't go back and read the previously written chapters until I finished the entire book. Then and only then would I read the book in its entirety. This kept me on track writing consistently and not just reading.

Frequently Asked Questions

How hard is it to write a book?
Writing a book is only as hard as you make it. If you plan the writing journey, the process becomes much easier for you. Don't get caught up on writing like an English Professor, write how you write and allow your editor to fix what needs to be fixed. Writing is not hard unless you make it hard. Plan your writing journey by outlining well.

How many words or pages should be in a chapter?
There is no set number of words or pages that should be included in a chapter. How many of each determines what you need to say to get your point across, to tell your story, to deliver your message. Think about the shortest chapter in the Bible, few words that would not even fill up 1 page, and the longest chapter, well its longer than the shortest. You decide what is needed in word count and you decide how many pages in each chapter. You may have some short chapters in your book and some long chapters. Either way, focus on what you are writing and be sure to write great content.

How many chapters should be in a book?
When I start planning to write a new book I never associate a number of chapters until after I outline and decide what should be included in the book. From there, I decide how many chapters based on the content and how it should be divided. There is no base number of chapters you should have. Focus on the content. As long as your readers get what was intended for them receive from the book that is what matters. 12 chapters or 60, you decide what you need.

Should I write in 1st or 3rd person?
My advice would be for you to think about other books you have read, think about how you verbally tell a story best, think about how you would like to read a book, then decide how you want to write a book, 1st or 3rd person. Be consistent when you write your story unless it makes sense to switch back and forth and your readers will understand your writing method.

Book Page Layout

The pages here are a general example of how to setup your book pages before you publish. Page 1 is the right side of the book, page 2 is the left side of the book.

When starting a new page, do not use the space key or tab key to get to the next page. Instead, insert a page break by going to the insert tab. Do this with every new page and to start each chapter. This will eliminate moving your content around if additional content is added or deleted.

	Blank	Blank
	Title	Blank
	Title Subtitle Author Name	Copyright

Dedication	Blank
Acknowledgment	Blank
Quote or Blank	Chapter 1

Writing Notes

Writing Notes

Writing Notes

Writing Notes

Writing Notes

Writing Notes

Writing Notes

Writing Notes

Writing Notes

Writing Notes

Writing Notes

Writing Notes

Writing Notes

Writing Notes

Writing Notes

Writing Notes

Writing Notes

Writing Notes

Writing Notes

Writing Notes

Project Title

_____

_____

_____

_____

_____

_____

Start Date_____

Completion Date_____

Outlining really is Everything!

This Book Belongs to

_____

Author Name (Pen Name)
Potential

_____
_____
_____
_____

Book Title & Sub Title
Potential

_____
_____
_____
_____

Know Your Why!

Why Statement

Idea Statement

Idea Statement

Brainstorm

Brainstorm

Research

Research

Story Summary

Story Summary

Story Summary

Story Summary

Story Summary

Commitment & Planning

Build Your Time Schedule

_____ Hours of sleep every night – Approximate average

_____ Hours of School/Work prep –morning/night, yourself and your children

_____ Hours of television – Weekly shows, other people watching TV that you get caught up in, Movies & etc.

_____ Hours of Relax "Me" time – Baths, naps, chill, phone, social media (non-working time), etc.

_____ Hours of Football/Basketball Time or other sports - kids practice to and from time, Game Day, watching sports, NBA/NFL on or going to games.

_____ Hours of 9-5 job or whatever your full time or part time job hours are. Include travel time there and back.

_____ Hours of spouse time. Don't include time already added for movies, chill time or any event that you two may be at together already listed above.

_____ Hours of kid time for whatever they need; help with homework, cook, etc. This is in addition to the time spent with them while doing other stuff such as school prep, football time, tv time, etc.

_____ Other time allotted for specifics in your life add here

_____
_____
_____
_____
_____
_____
_____
_____
_____
_____

_____ Add the previous page numbers together to come up with your total. Add it below.

_____ This is your total Hours of Occupied time in a week. Above totals.

168 hours (7-day work week total hours) - (minus) Total Occupied Hours = _____ hours.

This is how many hours remaining in your week that you can dedicate to your writing and accomplishing your dreams of publishing a book. Think about the time you mentioned above that is dedicated to other items. Besides sleep, unless it's more than 8 hours a night, think of what you can exclude to give yourself more time to write.

When multi-tasking with the time above, you could find additional time to add to your week to make time to write consistently. Any idol time is additional time that can be used towards your dream. Down town at work, sitting, waiting at practice, etc. So now you have an idea of how much time you have available to commit to writing.

YOU HAVE APPROXIMATELY _____ HOURS A WEEK TO WRITE!

YOU HAVE APPROXIMATELY _____ HOURS A WEEK TO DEDICATE TO WRITING!

Commitment Pledge

I _____
am committing to write _____ hours a week and _____ days a week.

Anything above and beyond will be a bonus! I pledge to commit to my writing and commit to myself because I am worthy!

Signed_____

Key Point Snippets

➢ 1. _____
_____
_____
_____

➢ 2. _____
_____
_____
_____

➢ 3. _____
_____
_____
_____

➢ 4. _____
_____
_____
_____

➢ 5. _____
_____
_____
_____

➢ 6. _____
_____
_____
_____

➢ 7. _____
_____
_____
_____

➢ 8. _____
_____
_____
_____

➢ 9. _____
_____
_____
_____

Key Point Snippets

➢ 10. _____
_____
_____

➢ 11. _____
_____
_____

➢ 12. _____
_____
_____

➢ 13. _____
_____
_____

➢ 14. _____
_____
_____

➢ 15. _____
_____
_____

➢ 16. _____
_____
_____

➢ 17. _____
_____
_____

➢ 18. _____
_____
_____

Key Point Snippets

➢ 19. _____
_____
_____

➢ 20. _____
_____
_____

➢ 21. _____
_____
_____

➢ 22. _____
_____
_____

➢ 23. _____
_____
_____

➢ 24. _____
_____
_____

➢ 25. _____
_____
_____

➢ 26. _____
_____
_____

➢ 27. _____
_____
_____

Key Point Snippets

- 28. _____

- 29. _____

- 30. _____

- 31. _____

- 32. _____

- 33. _____

- 34. _____

- 35. _____

- 36. _____

Key Point Snippets

➢ 37. _____

➢ 38. _____

➢ 39. _____

➢ 40. _____

➢ 41. _____

➢ 42. _____

➢ 43. _____

➢ 44. _____

➢ 45. _____

Key Point Details

Key Point #

Key Point #

Key Point #

Key Point #

Key Point Details

Key Point #	Key Point #
Key Point #	Key Point #

Key Point Details

Key Point #

Key Point #

Key Point #

Key Point #

Key Point Details

Key Point #

Key Point #

Key Point #

Key Point #

Character Name Brainstorm

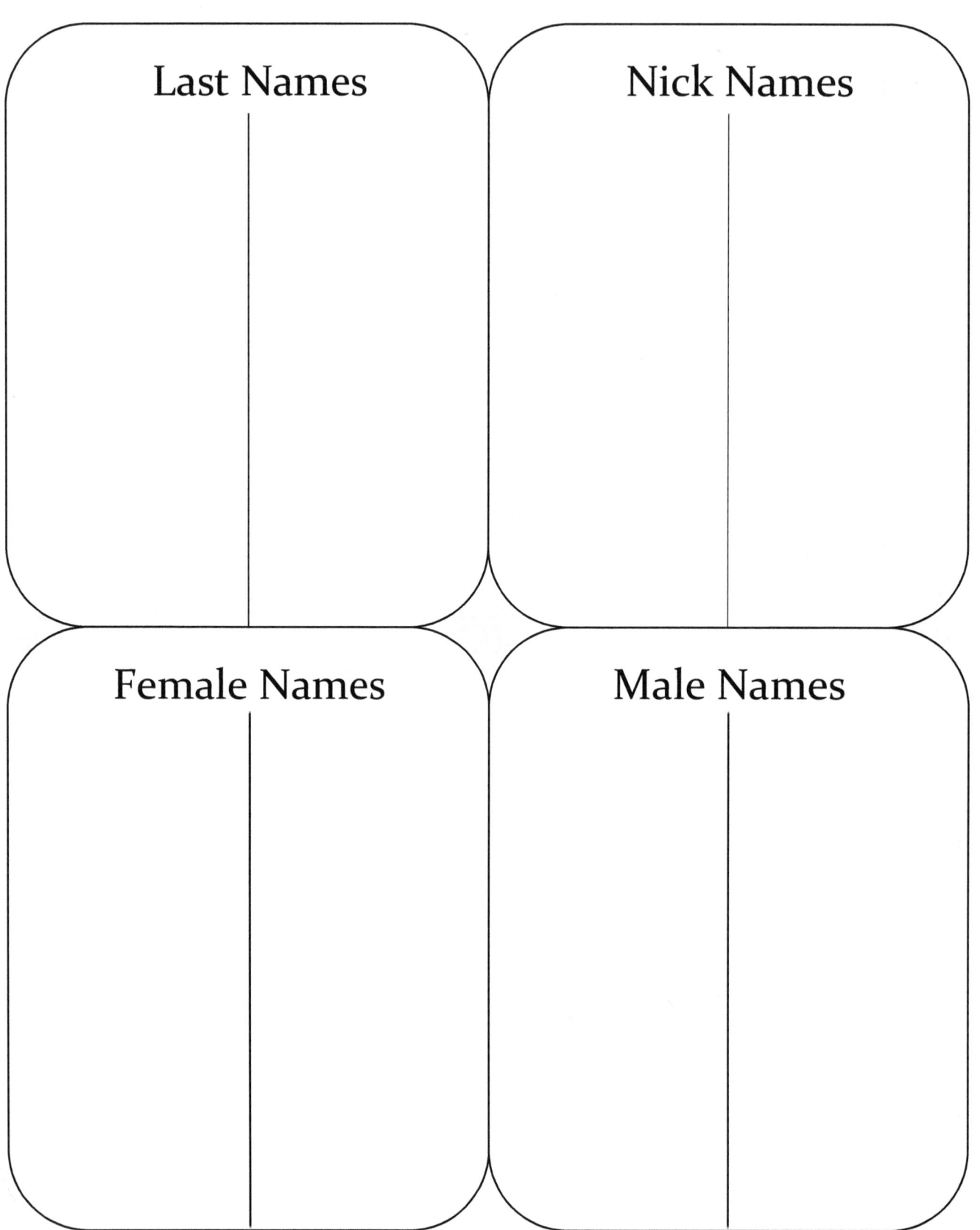

Character Profile

Name _____
Nick Name _____ Social Status _____
Age _____ Birthday _____
Height _____ Race _____ Sex _____
Weight _____ Religion _____

Body Type _____
_____
Body Assets (big butt, boobs,
muscular, basketball build, etc) ____
_____
_____
_____
_____
Personality _____
_____
_____
Dress style _____
_____
Other _____
_____
_____
_____

Character Description _____
_____
_____
_____
_____
Purpose in Story _____
_____
_____
_____
Plots planned for Character _____
_____
_____
_____
_____

Lifestyle _____
Income class _____
House _____
Car drive _____
Neighborhood _____
Kids _____
Siblings _____
Parents _____
Other relatives _____
Friends _____
Favorite Music _____
Favorite Saying _____
Other _____
_____

Sequel Setup/Cliffhangers _____
_____
_____
_____
Important Dates _____
_____
Secrets _____
_____
_____
Character Key Points _____
_____
_____
_____

Additional Notes:

Character Profile

Name_____
Nick Name_____ Social Status _____
Age_____ Birthday_____
Height_____ Race _____Sex_____
Weight_____ Religion

Body Type _____
_____
Body Assets (big butt, boobs,
muscular, basketball build, etc)_____
_____
_____
_____
Personality_____
_____
_____
Dress style _____
_____
Other _____
_____
_____
_____

Character Description_____
_____
_____
_____
_____
Purpose in Story_____
_____
_____
_____
Plots planned for Character_____
_____
_____
_____
_____

Lifestyle_____
Income class_____
House_____
Car drive_____
Neighborhood_____
Kids_____
Siblings_____
Parents_____
Other relatives_____
Friends_____
Favorite Music_____
Favorite Saying_____
Other_____
_____
_____

Sequel Setup/Cliffhangers_____
_____
_____
_____
Important Dates _____
_____
_____
Secrets _____
_____
_____
_____
Character Key Points_____
_____
_____
_____

Additional Notes:

Character Profile

Name_____
Nick Name_____ Social Status _____
Age_____ Birthday_____
Height_____ Race _____ Sex_____
Weight_____ Religion_____

Body Type _____

Body Assets (big butt, boobs, muscular, basketball build, etc)_____
_____
_____
_____

Personality_____
_____

Dress style _____

Other _____
_____
_____

Character Description_____
_____
_____
_____

Purpose in Story_____
_____
_____
_____

Plots planned for Character_____
_____
_____
_____

Lifestyle_____
Income class_____
House_____
Car drive_____
Neighborhood_____
Kids_____
Siblings_____
Parents_____
Other relatives_____
Friends_____
Favorite Music_____
Favorite Saying_____
Other_____
_____
_____

Sequel Setup/Cliffhangers_____
_____
_____

Important Dates _____
_____

Secrets _____
_____

Character Key Points_____
_____
_____
_____

Additional Notes:

Character Profile

Name_____
Nick Name_____ Social Status _____
Age_____ Birthday_____
Height_____ Race _____ Sex_____
Weight_____ Religion_____

Body Type _____
_____
Body Assets (big butt, boobs,
muscular, basketball build, etc)_____
_____
_____
_____
Personality_____
_____
_____
Dress style _____
_____
Other _____
_____
_____

Lifestyle_____
Income class_____
House_____
Car drive_____
Neighborhood_____
Kids_____
Siblings_____
Parents_____
Other relatives_____
Friends_____
Favorite Music_____
Favorite Saying_____
Other_____
_____

Character Description_____
_____
_____
_____
_____
Purpose in Story_____
_____
_____
_____
_____
Plots planned for Character_____
_____
_____
_____
_____

Sequel Setup/Cliffhangers_____
_____
_____
_____
Important Dates _____
_____
_____
Secrets _____
_____
_____
_____
Character Key Points_____
_____
_____
_____

Additional Notes:

Character Profile

Name_____
Nick Name_____ Social Status _____
Age_____ Birthday_____
Height_____ Race _____ Sex_____
Weight_____ Religion_____

Body Type _____
_____
Body Assets (big butt, boobs,
muscular, basketball build, etc)_____
_____
_____
_____
Personality_____
_____
_____
Dress style _____
_____
Other _____
_____
_____
_____

Lifestyle_____
Income class_____
House_____
Car drive_____
Neighborhood_____
Kids_____
Siblings_____
Parents_____
Other relatives_____
Friends_____
Favorite Music_____
Favorite Saying_____
Other_____
_____

Character Description_____
_____
_____
_____
_____
Purpose in Story_____
_____
_____
_____
Plots planned for Character_____
_____
_____
_____
_____

Sequel Setup/Cliffhangers_____
_____
_____
_____
Important Dates _____
_____
Secrets _____
_____
_____
Character Key Points_____
_____
_____
_____

Additional Notes:

Character Profile

Name_____
Nick Name_____ Social Status _____
Age_____ Birthday_____
Height_____ Race _____ Sex_____
Weight_____ Religion_____

Body Type _____
_____
Body Assets (big butt, boobs, muscular, basketball build, etc)_____
_____
_____
_____
Personality_____
_____
_____
Dress style_____
_____
Other _____
_____
_____
_____

Character Description_____
_____
_____
_____
_____
Purpose in Story_____
_____
_____
_____
Plots planned for Character_____
_____
_____
_____
_____

Lifestyle_____
Income class_____
House_____
Car drive_____
Neighborhood_____
Kids_____
Siblings_____
Parents_____
Other relatives_____
Friends_____
Favorite Music_____
Favorite Saying_____
Other_____
_____
_____

Sequel Setup/Cliffhangers_____
_____
_____
_____
Important Dates _____
_____
Secrets _____
_____
_____
Character Key Points_____
_____
_____
_____

Additional Notes:

Character Profile

Name_____
Nick Name_____ Social Status _____
Age_____ Birthday_____
Height_____ Race _____ Sex_____
Weight_____ Religion_____

Body Type _____
_____
Body Assets (big butt, boobs,
muscular, basketball build, etc)_____
_____
_____
_____
Personality_____
_____
_____
Dress style _____
Other _____
_____
_____
_____

Lifestyle_____
Income class_____
House_____
Car drive_____
Neighborhood_____
Kids_____
Siblings_____
Parents_____
Other relatives_____
Friends_____
Favorite Music_____
Favorite Saying_____
Other_____
_____
_____

Character Description_____
_____
_____
_____
_____
_____
Purpose in Story_____
_____
_____
_____
Plots planned for Character_____
_____
_____
_____
_____

Sequel Setup/Cliffhangers_____
_____
_____
_____
Important Dates _____
_____
Secrets _____
_____
_____
Character Key Points_____
_____
_____
_____
_____

Additional Notes:

Character Profile

Name_____
Nick Name_____ Social Status _____
Age_____ Birthday_____
Height_____ Race _____ Sex_____
Weight_____ Religion

Body Type _____

Body Assets (big butt, boobs, muscular, basketball build, etc)_____
_____
_____

Personality_____
_____
_____

Dress style _____

Other _____
_____
_____

Lifestyle_____
Income class_____
House_____
Car drive_____
Neighborhood_____
Kids_____
Siblings_____
Parents_____
Other relatives_____
Friends_____
Favorite Music_____
Favorite Saying_____
Other_____
_____

Character Description_____
_____
_____
_____

Purpose in Story_____
_____
_____
_____

Plots planned for Character_____
_____
_____
_____
_____

Sequel Setup/Cliffhangers_____
_____
_____

Important Dates _____
_____

Secrets _____
_____
_____

Character Key Points_____
_____
_____
_____

Additional Notes:

Character Relationships

Main Character	Main Character
_____	_____

Family Members

_____   _____
_____   _____
_____   _____
_____   _____
_____   _____

Love Interest

_____   _____
_____   _____
_____   _____

Business Relationships

_____   _____
_____   _____
_____   _____

Other Character Relationships

_____   _____
_____   _____
_____   _____
_____   _____

Character Relationships

Main Character
_____

Family Members
_____
_____
_____
_____
_____
_____

Love Interest
_____
_____
_____
_____

Business Relationships
_____
_____
_____
_____

Other Character Relationships
_____
_____
_____
_____

Main Character
_____

Family Members
_____
_____
_____
_____
_____
_____

Love Interest
_____
_____
_____
_____

Business Relationships
_____
_____
_____
_____

Other Character Relationships
_____
_____
_____
_____

Character Relationships

Main Character | Main Character
_____ | _____

Family Members | Family Members
_____ | _____
_____ | _____
_____ | _____
_____ | _____
_____ | _____

Love Interest | Love Interest
_____ | _____
_____ | _____
_____ | _____
_____ | _____

Business Relationships | Business Relationships
_____ | _____
_____ | _____
_____ | _____
_____ | _____

Other Character Relationships | Other Character Relationships
_____ | _____
_____ | _____
_____ | _____
_____ | _____

Character Relationships

Main Character

_____

Family Members

_____
_____
_____
_____
_____

Love Interest

_____
_____
_____
_____

Business Relationships

_____
_____
_____
_____

Other Character Relationships

_____
_____
_____
_____
_____

Main Character

_____

Family Members

_____
_____
_____
_____
_____

Love Interest

_____
_____
_____
_____

Business Relationships

_____
_____
_____
_____

Other Character Relationships

_____
_____
_____
_____
_____

Sub-Character Quick Snapshot

***Name _____ Nickname _____
Age _____ Gender _____ Height _____ Race _____
Characteristics _____
Character relations _____
Purpose in story _____
_____
_____
_____

***Name _____ Nickname _____
Age _____ Gender _____ Height _____ Race _____
Characteristics _____
Character relations _____
Purpose in story _____
_____
_____
_____

***Name _____ Nickname _____
Age _____ Gender _____ Height _____ Race _____
Characteristics _____
Character relations _____
Purpose in story _____
_____
_____
_____

***Name _____ Nickname _____
Age _____ Gender _____ Height _____ Race _____
Characteristics _____
Character relations _____
Purpose in story _____
_____
_____
_____

***Name _____ Nickname _____
Age _____ Gender _____ Height _____ Race _____
Characteristics _____
Character relations _____
Purpose in story _____
_____
_____
_____

Sub-Character Quick Snapshot

***Name _____ Nickname _____
Age _____ Gender _____ Height _____ Race _____
Characteristics_____
Character relations _____
Purpose in story_____
_____
_____
_____

***Name _____ Nickname _____
Age _____ Gender _____ Height _____ Race _____
Characteristics_____
Character relations _____
Purpose in story_____
_____
_____
_____

***Name _____ Nickname _____
Age _____ Gender _____ Height _____ Race _____
Characteristics_____
Character relations _____
Purpose in story_____
_____
_____
_____

***Name _____ Nickname _____
Age _____ Gender _____ Height _____ Race _____
Characteristics_____
Character relations _____
Purpose in story_____
_____
_____
_____

***Name _____ Nickname _____
Age _____ Gender _____ Height _____ Race _____
Characteristics_____
Character relations _____
Purpose in story_____
_____
_____
_____

Character Table of Content

Name	Character Description

Time Capsule

List the sequence of events that take place in the story.

Time Capsule

List the sequence of events that take place in the story.

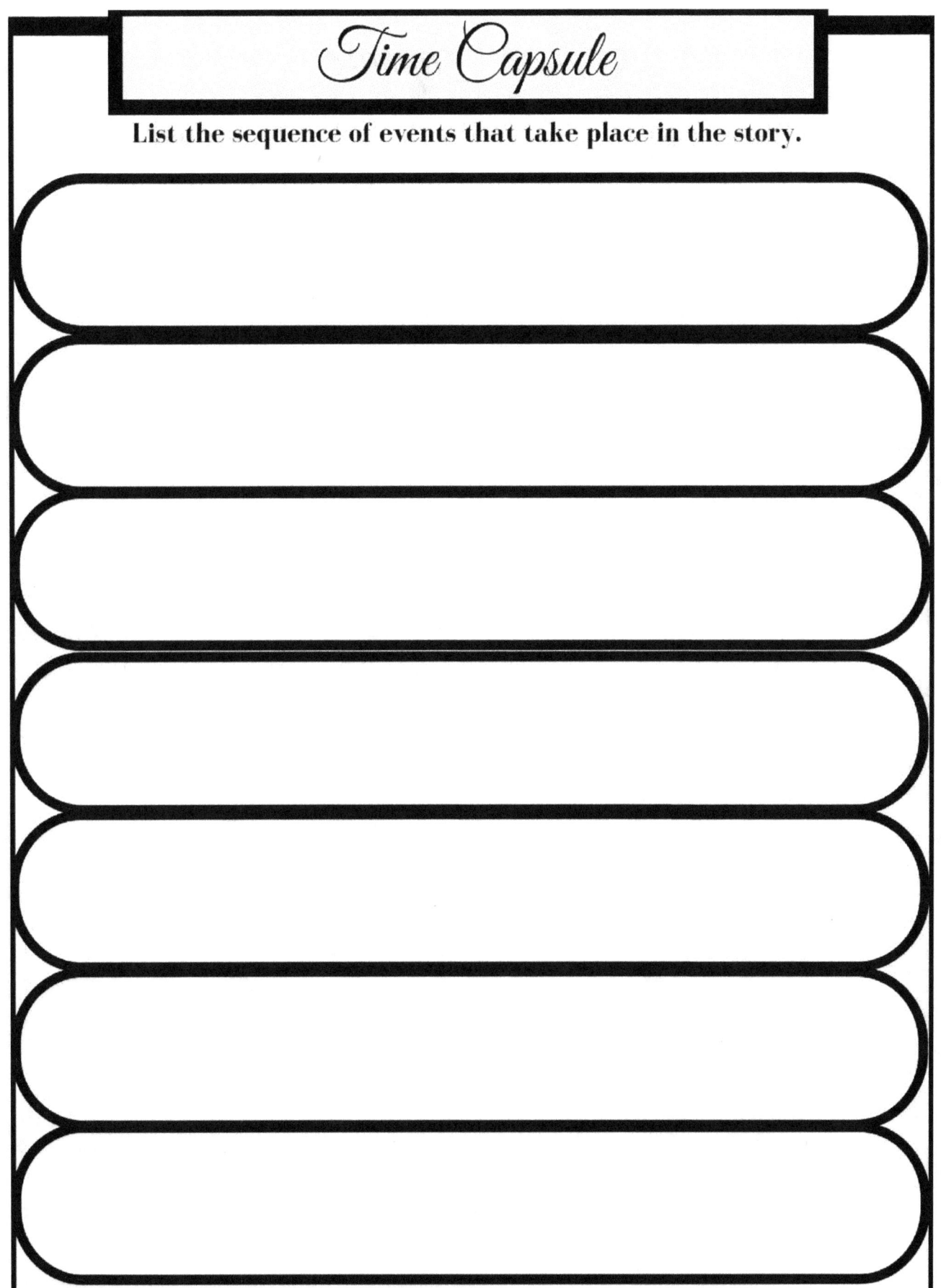

Time Capsule

List the sequence of events that take place in the story.

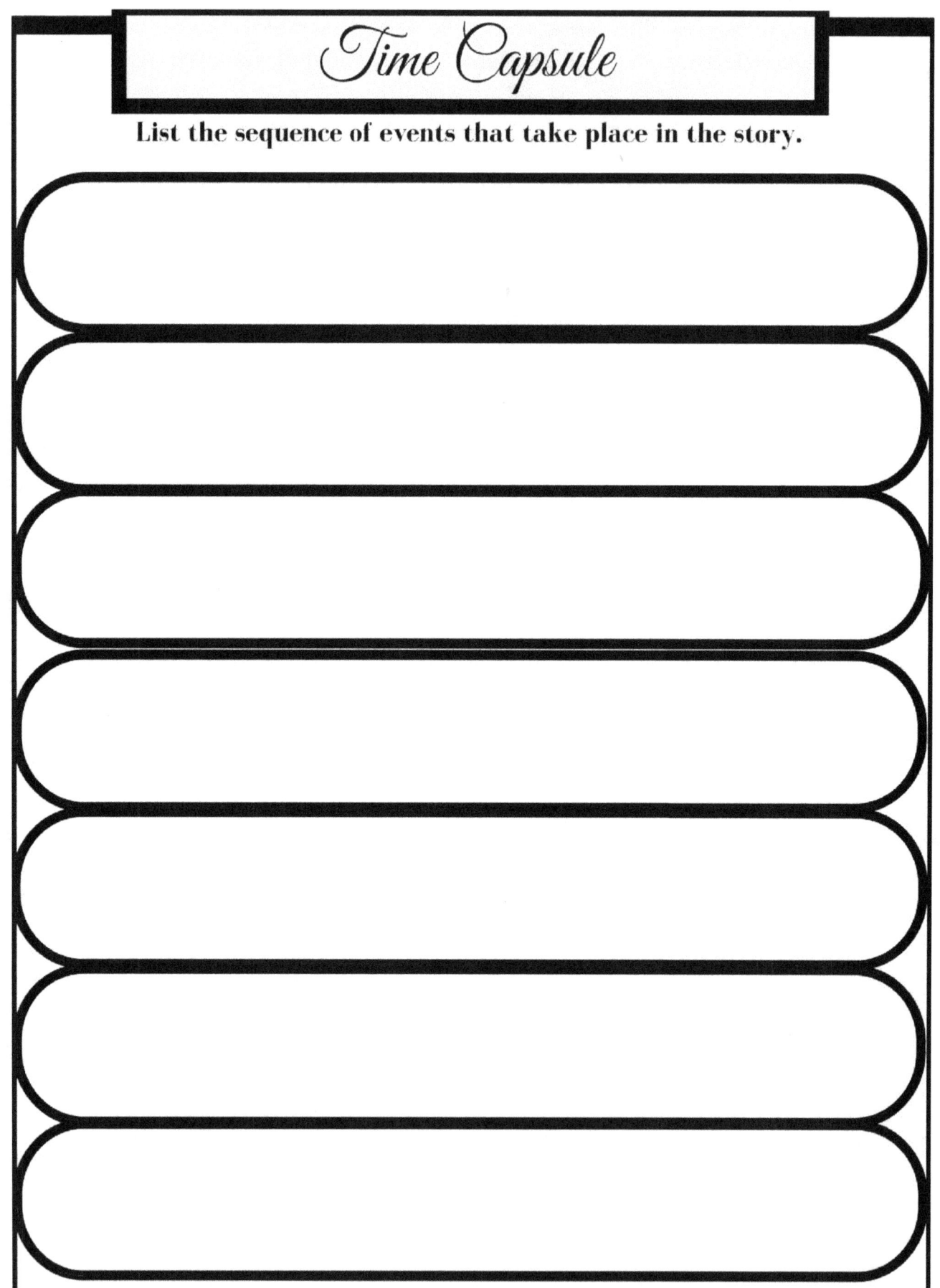

Chapter Table of Content

1. ___
2. ___
3. ___
4. ___
5. ___
6. ___
7. ___
8. ___
9. ___
10. ___
11. ___
12. ___
13. ___
14. ___
15. ___

Chapter Table of Content

16. _____
17. _____
18. _____
19. _____
20. _____
21. _____
22. _____
23. _____
24. _____
25. _____
26. _____
27. _____
28. _____
29. _____
30. _____

Chapter Table of Content

31.
32.
33.
34.
35.
36.
37.
38.
39.
40.
41.
42.
43.
44.
45.

Chapter Summary

1.
2.
3.
4.
5.
6.
7.

Additional Notes

Chapter Summary

8.

9.

10.

11.

12.

13.

14.

Additional Notes

Chapter Summary

15

16

17

18

19

20

21

Additional

Chapter Summary

22

23

24

25

26

27

28

Additional

Chapter Summary

29

30

31

32

33

34

35

Additional

Chapter Summary

36

37

38

39

40

41

42

Additional

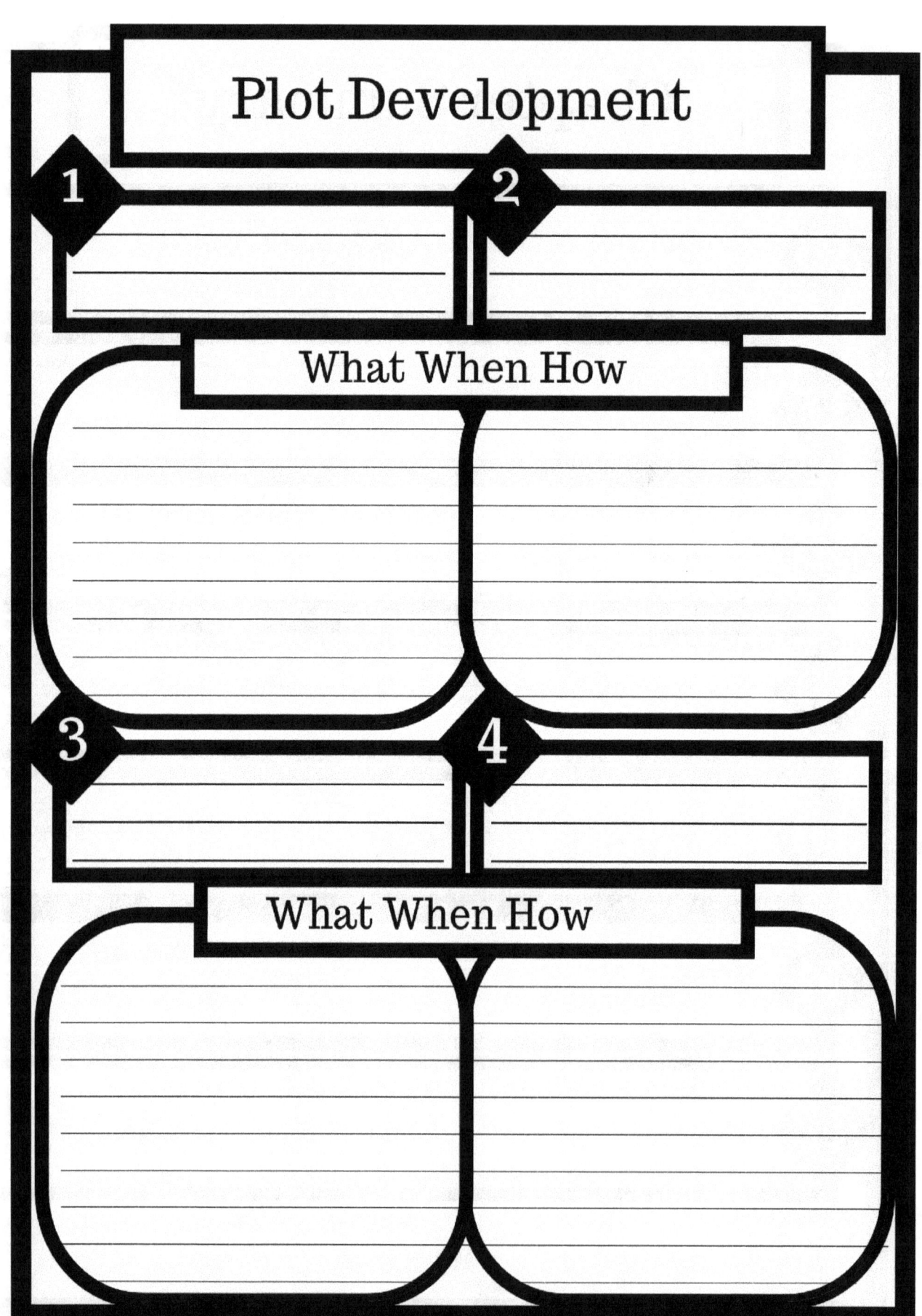

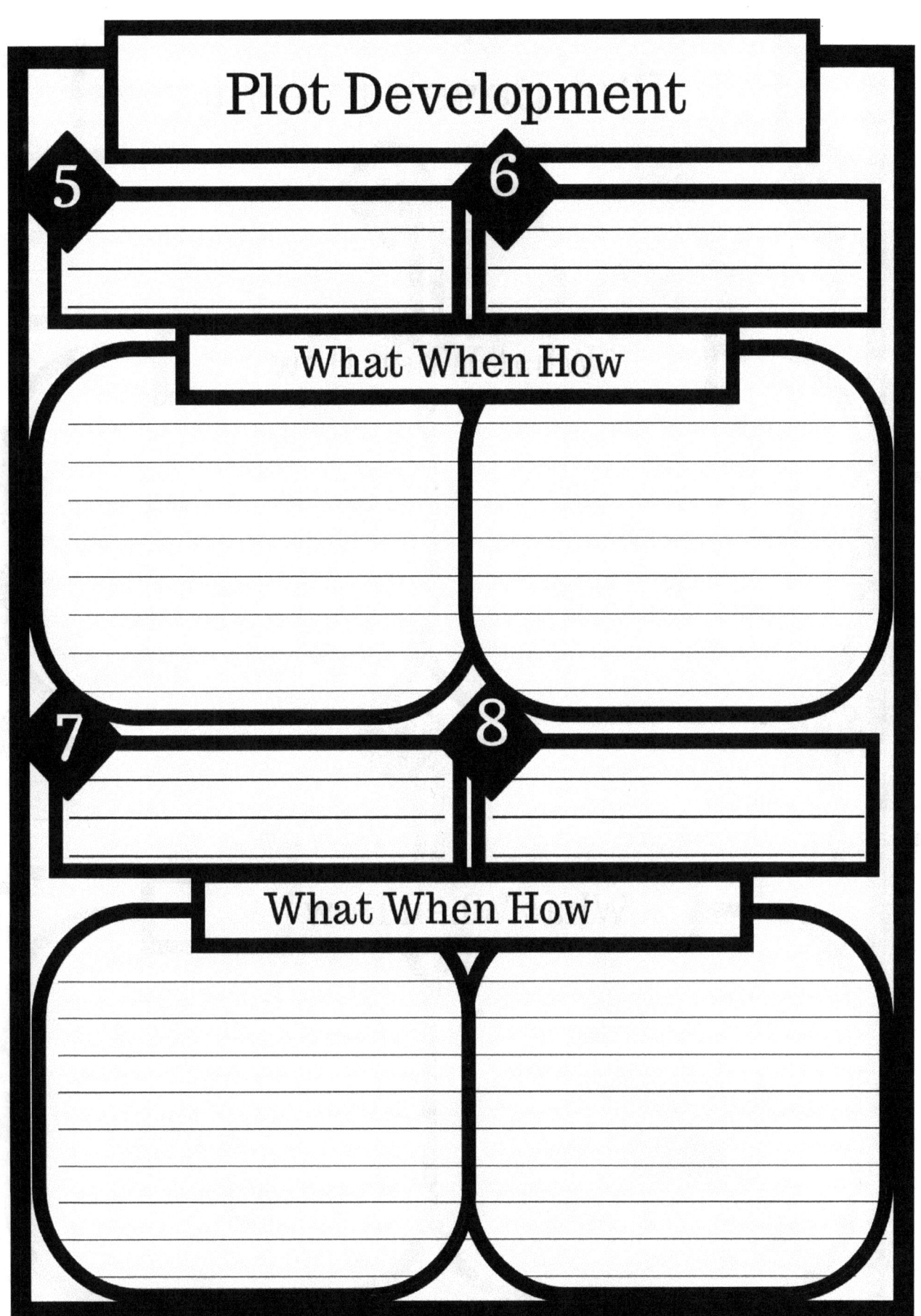

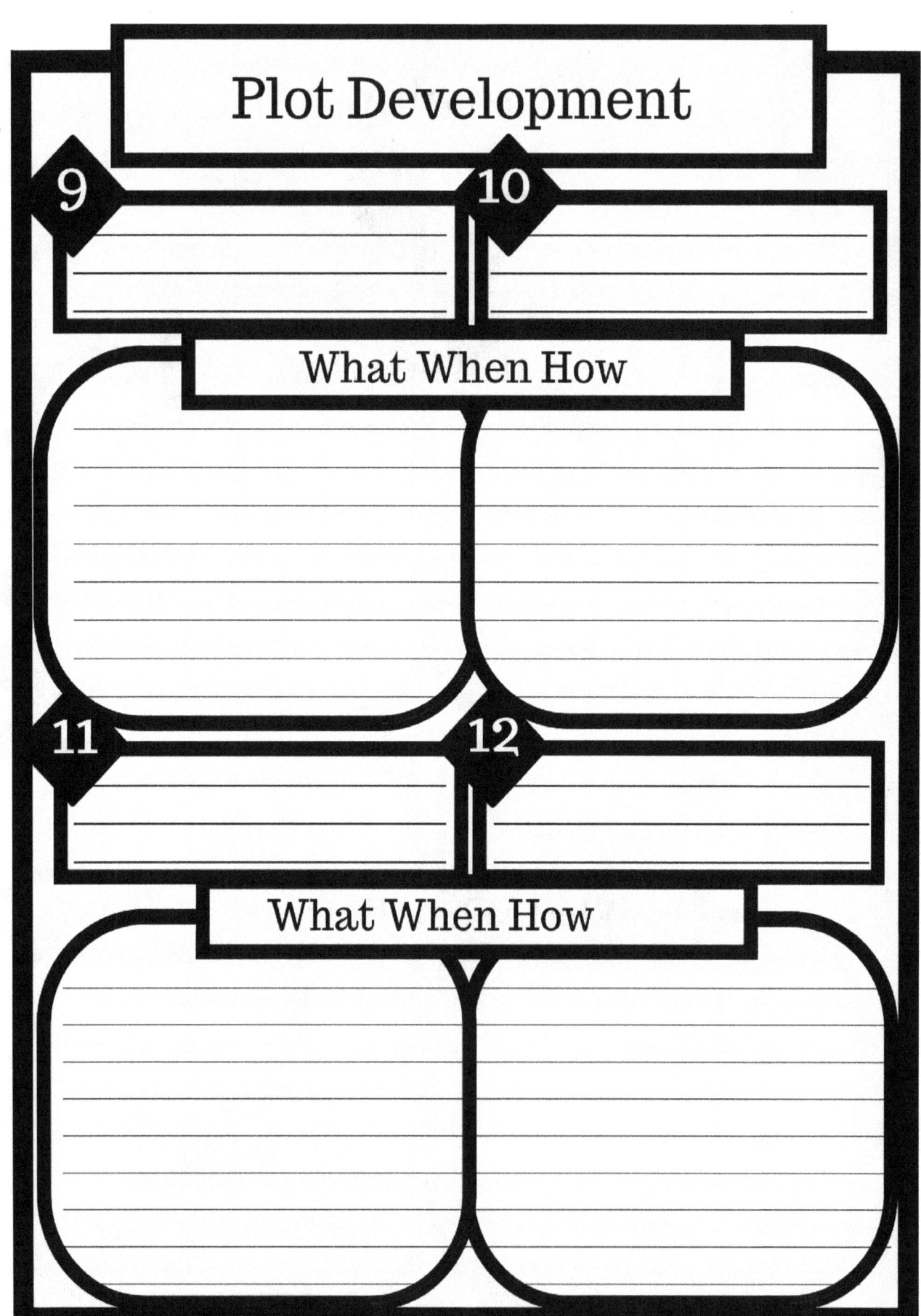

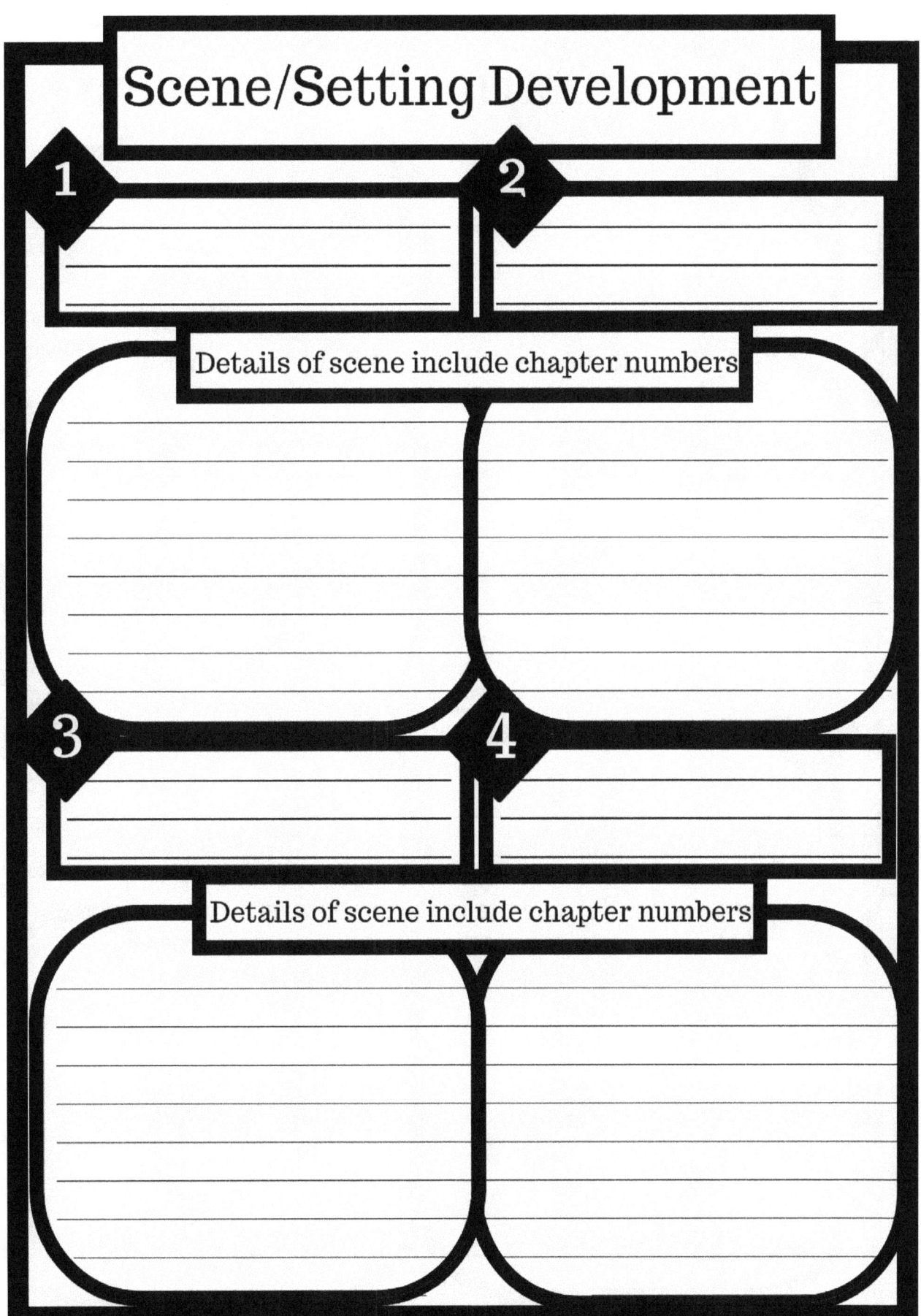

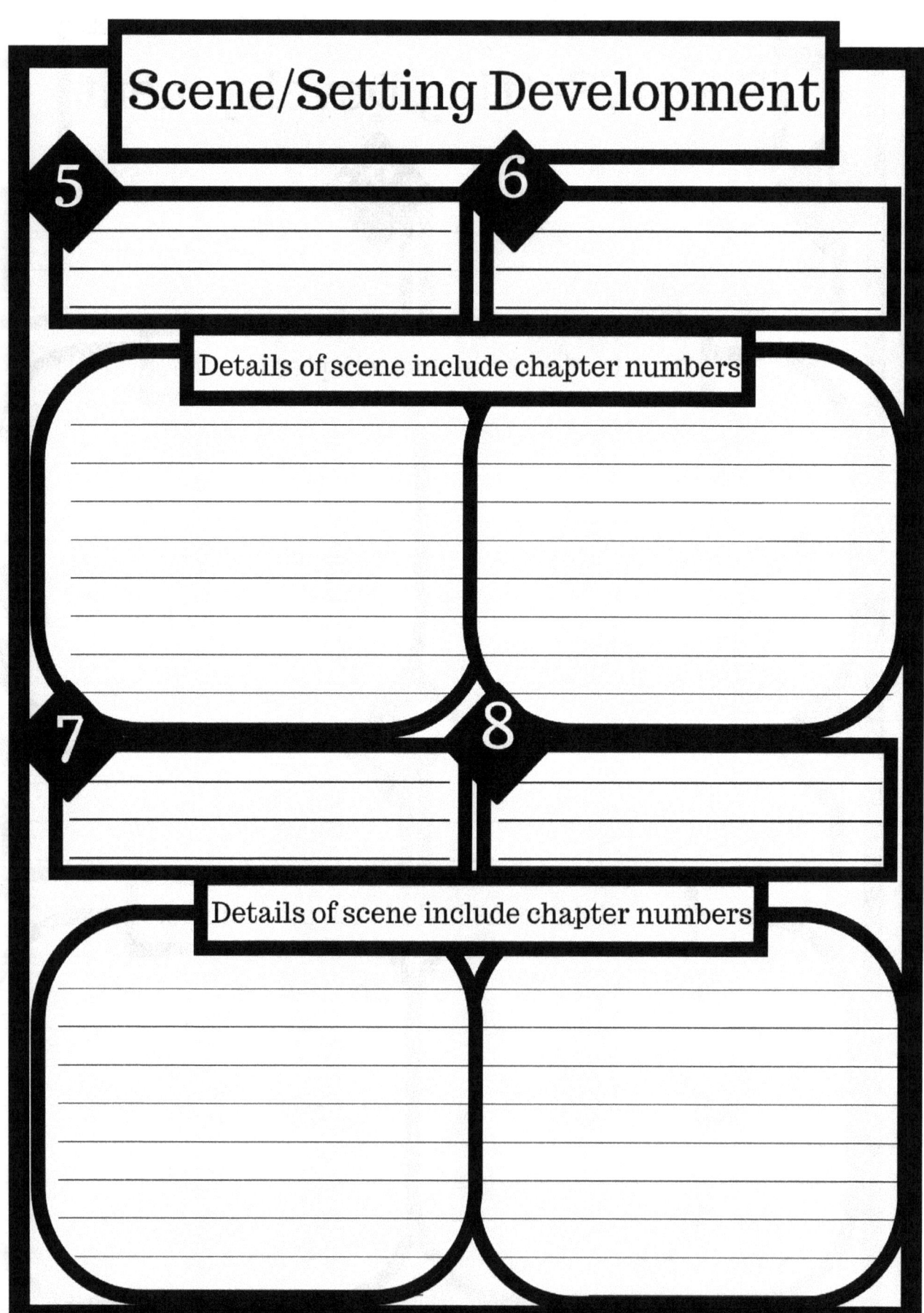

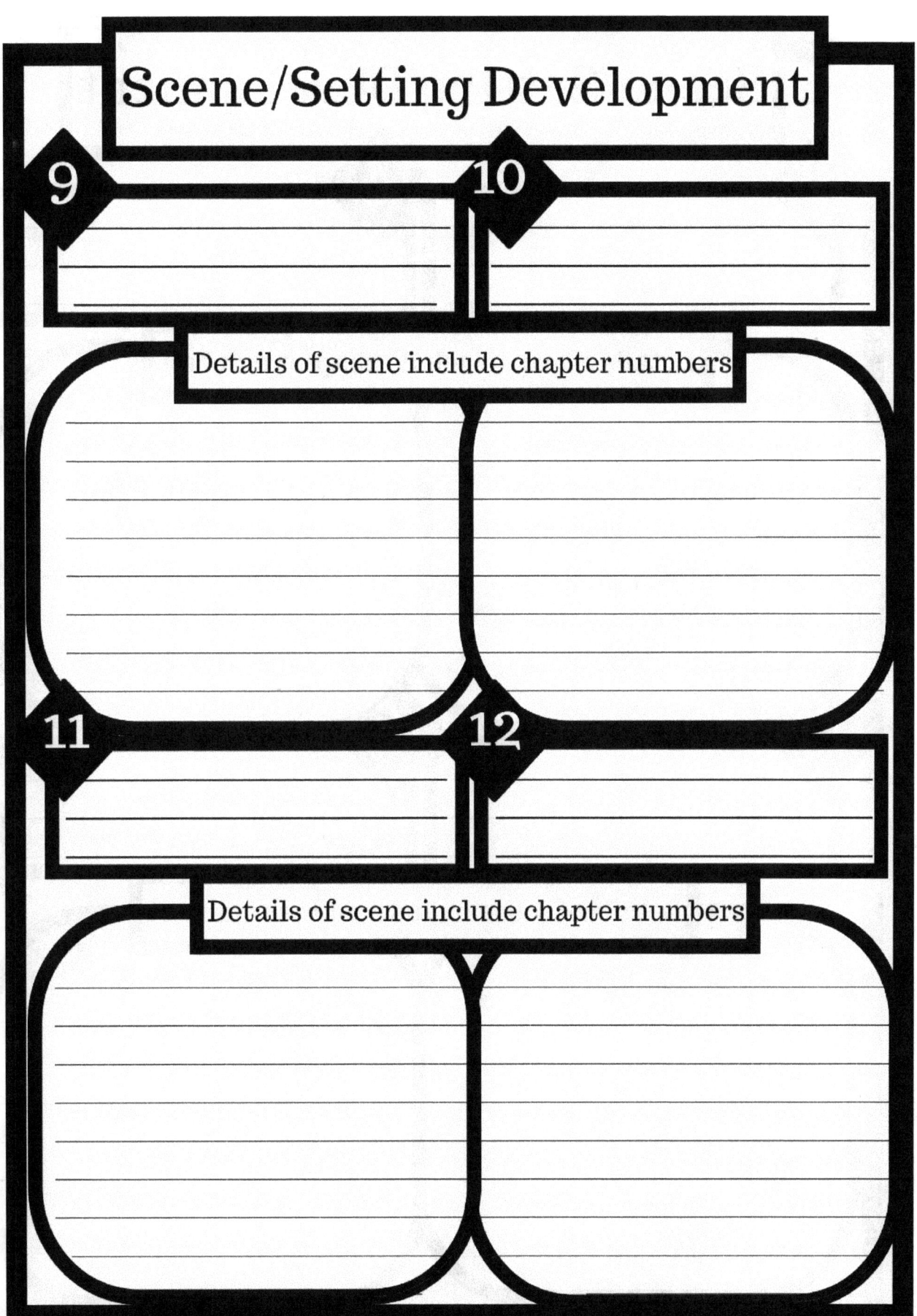

Scene/Setting Development

13

14

Details of scene include chapter numbers

15

16

Details of scene include chapter numbers

Writing First Chapter

First Chapter Characters _____

_____
_____
_____
_____
_____
_____
_____

First Chapter Attention Grabber Scenes_____

_____
_____
_____
_____
_____
_____
_____

First Chapter Plot Introduction Setup _____

_____
_____
_____
_____
_____
_____
_____
_____
_____
_____
_____

First Chapter Notes _____

_____
_____
_____
_____
_____
_____
_____

Sequel Setup

Sequel Idea _____

_____
_____
_____
_____
_____
_____

Sequel Plots, Twist & Turns _____

_____
_____
_____
_____
_____
_____
_____

Sequel Setup _____

_____
_____
_____
_____
_____
_____
_____
_____
_____
_____
_____

Sequel Notes _____

_____
_____
_____
_____
_____

27 Day Writing Plan

Day 1
Day 2
Day 3
Day 4

Day 5
Day 6
Day 7
Day 8
Day 9
Day 10
Day 11

Day 12
Day 13
Day 14
Day 15
Day 16
Day 17
Day 18
Day 19

Day 20
Day 21
Day 22
Day 23
Day 24
Day 25
Day 26
Day 27

After Completing 27 Day Writing Challenge whats left?
*
*
*
*
*
*
*

Additional Notes:

27 Day Writing Plan

Day 1
Day 2
Day 3
Day 4

Day 5
Day 6
Day 7
Day 8
Day 9
Day 10
Day 11

Day 12
Day 13
Day 14
Day 15
Day 16
Day 17
Day 18
Day 19

Day 20
Day 21
Day 22
Day 23
Day 24
Day 25
Day 26
Day 27

After Completing 27 Day Writing Challenge whats left?
*
*
*
*
*
*
*

Additional Notes:

01
Daily Word Goal

Beginning Word Count

Ending Word Count

Total Word Goal Met

Total Word Goal Un-Met

02
Daily Word Goal

Beginning Word Count

Ending Word Count

Total Word Goal Met

Total Word Goal Un-Met

03
Daily Word Goal

Beginning Word Count

Ending Word Count

Total Word Goal Met

Total Word Goal Un-Met

04
Daily Word Goal

Beginning Word Count

Ending Word Count

Total Word Goal Met

Total Word Goal Un-Met

05
Daily Word Goal

Beginning Word Count

Ending Word Count

Total Word Goal Met

Total Word Goal Un-Met

06
Daily Word Goal

Beginning Word Count

Ending Word Count

Total Word Goal Met

Total Word Goal Un-Met

Week _____ *of* _____ *Completed* _____

07
Total Weekly Word Goal _____
Word Goal Met _____
Total Un-Met Word Goal _____
Make up Word Goal _____
Word Goal Met _____

01
Daily Word Goal

Beginning Word Count

Ending Word Count

Total Word Goal Met

Total Word Goal Un-Met

02
Daily Word Goal

Beginning Word Count

Ending Word Count

Total Word Goal Met

Total Word Goal Un-Met

03
Daily Word Goal

Beginning Word Count

Ending Word Count

Total Word Goal Met

Total Word Goal Un-Met

04
Daily Word Goal

Beginning Word Count

Ending Word Count

Total Word Goal Met

Total Word Goal Un-Met

05
Daily Word Goal

Beginning Word Count

Ending Word Count

Total Word Goal Met

Total Word Goal Un-Met

06
Daily Word Goal

Beginning Word Count

Ending Word Count

Total Word Goal Met

Total Word Goal Un-Met

Week _____ of _____ Completed _____

07
Total Weekly Word Goal _____
Word Goal Met _____
Total Un-Met Word Goal _____
Make up Word Goal _____
Word Goal Met _____

01

Daily Word Goal

Beginning Word Count

Ending Word Count

Total Word Goal Met

Total Word Goal Un-Met

02

Daily Word Goal

Beginning Word Count

Ending Word Count

Total Word Goal Met

Total Word Goal Un-Met

03

Daily Word Goal

Beginning Word Count

Ending Word Count

Total Word Goal Met

Total Word Goal Un-Met

04

Daily Word Goal

Beginning Word Count

Ending Word Count

Total Word Goal Met

Total Word Goal Un-Met

05

Daily Word Goal

Beginning Word Count

Ending Word Count

Total Word Goal Met

Total Word Goal Un-Met

06

Daily Word Goal

Beginning Word Count

Ending Word Count

Total Word Goal Met

Total Word Goal Un-Met

Week _____ *of* _____ *Completed* _____

07

Total Weekly Word Goal _____

Word Goal Met _____

Total Un-Met Word Goal _____

Make up Word Goal _____

Word Goal Met _____

01
Daily Word Goal

Beginning Word Count

Ending Word Count

Total Word Goal Met

Total Word Goal Un-Met

02
Daily Word Goal

Beginning Word Count

Ending Word Count

Total Word Goal Met

Total Word Goal Un-Met

03
Daily Word Goal

Beginning Word Count

Ending Word Count

Total Word Goal Met

Total Word Goal Un-Met

04
Daily Word Goal

Beginning Word Count

Ending Word Count

Total Word Goal Met

Total Word Goal Un-Met

05
Daily Word Goal

Beginning Word Count

Ending Word Count

Total Word Goal Met

Total Word Goal Un-Met

06
Daily Word Goal

Beginning Word Count

Ending Word Count

Total Word Goal Met

Total Word Goal Un-Met

Week _____ of _____ Completed _____

07
Total Weekly Word Goal_____
Word Goal Met _____
Total Un-Met Word Goal_____
Make up Word Goal _____
Word Goal Met _____

Writing Mood / Music for Mood

Mood _____
_____
_____
_____

Mood _____
_____
_____
_____

Mood _____
_____
_____
_____

Mood _____
_____
_____
_____

Mood _____
_____
_____
_____

Mood _____
_____
_____
_____

Mood _____
_____
_____
_____

Music _____
_____
_____
_____

Music _____
_____
_____
_____

Music _____
_____
_____
_____

Music _____
_____
_____
_____

Music _____
_____
_____
_____

Music _____
_____
_____
_____

Music _____
_____
_____
_____

Snack List

Healthy Snacks

Feel Good Snacks

Beverages

More Feel Good Snacks

To Do List/Checklist

[] Start thinking about your book cover design. Find someone who can design you an amazing eye-catching cover that anyone would be tempted to pick up when they see your book on the shelf.

[] Think about the size you want your book to be 5x7, 6x9, etc. you decide.

[] Create you a social media account for your book/author name. Start marketing yourself and your book as soon as possible

[] Start marketing your book at least 30 days prior to your release date. Social Media, marketing plan, family & friends.

[] Think about what your brand is for your book and start branding yourself as you promote your book.

[] Research your publishing options. Traditional versus Self-publishing, Major publishing house versus Print on Demand like Amazon Creatspace or Ingram Sparks.

[] Get you an accountability partner who can check on your status and keep you on track with your writing.

[] Create a budget for expenses you may incur like book cover, editing, marketing, books to have on hand.

[] Do, do, do, and do some more. Write, write, write, and write some more. Yes you can!

[] Believe in yourself!

Writing Notes

Writing Notes

Writing Notes

Writing Notes

Writing Notes

Writing Notes

Writing Notes

Writing Notes

Writing Notes

Writing Notes

Writing Notes

Writing Notes

Writing Notes

Writing Notes

Writing Notes

Writing Notes

Writing Notes

Writing Notes

Writing Notes

Writing Notes

www.ingramcontent.com/pod-product-compliance
Lightning Source LLC
Chambersburg PA
CBHW081916170426
43200CB00014B/2746